STORYNSHIP

T0322825

Also Available From Bloomsbury

STORYING OUR RELATIONSHIP WITH NATURE

Educating the Heart and Cultivating Courage Amidst the Climate Crisis

Amanda Fiore and Jing Lin

BLOOMSBURY ACADEMIC
LONDON • NEW YORK • OXFORD • NEW DELHI • SYDNEY

BLOOMSBURY ACADEMIC
Bloomsbury Publishing Plc
50 Bedford Square, London, WC1B 3DP, UK
1385 Broadway, New York, NY 10018, USA
29 Earlsfort Terrace, Dublin 2, Ireland

BLOOMSBURY, BLOOMSBURY ACADEMIC and the Diana logo are trademarks
of Bloomsbury Publishing Plc

First published in Great Britain 2024

Cover image: Kings Canyon National Park, CA, United States © Larry Gerbrandt /
Getty Images

A catalogue record for this book is available from the British Library.

A catalog record for this book is available from the Library of Congress.

ISBN: HB: 978-1-3503-6137-9
PB: 978-1-3503-6136-2
ePDF: 978-1-3503-6138-6
eBook: 978-1-3503-6139-3

Typeset by Deanta Global Publishing Services, Chennai, India
Printed and bound in Great Britain

To find out more about our authors and books visit www.bloomsbury.com and
sign up for our newsletters.

CONTENTS

Act IV
"RESTORYING" FOR CHANGE: WHAT DOES IT MEAN AND HOW DOES IT WORK? (A BEGINNER'S GUIDE)

INTRODUCTION

Setting Our Sights on Love, Compassion, and Inner Wisdom

As we adjust to a world where billionaires launch into outer space, gazing upon the fragile atmosphere of our planet from their privately owned rockets, it has never been clearer how capable we are of accomplishing astounding feats, or how motivated we are by money. In these unheralded trips there is the mark of both remarkable power and deep insecurity—we yearn for the extraordinary. Extraordinary feats attract money, which underscores one of the central concerns of this book: that despite our seemingly boundless ingenuity, creativity, and determination, the bulk of our concern and attention remains consistently and firmly grounded in the accumulation of power and material things.

What if all the power of the human race was guided by a force of loving care rather than profit or wealth accumulation? What if the global economy rewarded the creation of peace and equality instead of cheap, disposable products, exclusive events, and exotic travel experiences? What if the environmental impacts of fuel and plastic were factored into their market price? What if we considered the state of the world, and determined that peaceful coexistence with all living beings, and a healthy future ecosystem, were more important than the conveniences of human beings? Given our current cultural imaginary, it may be difficult to conceive of such a place, so you will need to use your creative vision—what would such a world look, smell, and sound like? How would living in such a world feel inside your body?

This book is our (Amanda & Jing's) attempt to chart a path toward the realization of just such a place . . . one guided by the unprecedented human capacity for love and connection, which we believe has the power to eclipse all other human concerns when cultivated with purpose and intention. To get there, we will need to take a long, hard look inward, considering where we are now, how we got here, and the false construction of these seemingly rock-solid foundations. We will then need to rediscover the power of the heart, relearning how to honor our intuition and wisdom as legitimate ways of knowing, as well as how to love humans and nonhumans alike as equal beings. But above all, we will need the courage and determination to imagine a new way, and **story** that new way into existence.

Let's Put Aside the Debate: Starting from a Point of Agreement

This book is not entering into a debate about climate change. Many books have been written in hopes of convincing the unconvinced—this book is not another one of these. In fact, let us state up front, clearly and unequivocally, that we—Amanda and Jing—take as self-evident that the globalized society in which we currently reside is rife with inequalities, including a denigration of Mother Earth's blessings so callous and severe it has set the entire planet hurtling toward climate chaos. As far as we are concerned, the science regarding the human cause of this disaster is indisputable. We put that debate aside in these pages and choose to start from a point of agreement in the science. In so doing, we skip over the question of *if* there is a problem and focus on understanding and addressing the crisis.

We (Amanda and Jing) come to these pages as contemplative educators, activists, and qualitative researchers deeply invested in the development of a more just, equitable, and peaceful global society. We believe the climate crisis has come about due to a human-centered crisis of the heart and spirit, which has left us deeply out of balance. In the pages that follow, we explore this crisis of imbalance through a combination of personal story, research, and reflective writing, ultimately calling on the ancient tool of *restorying* as a powerful way to rediscover the balance we have lost and reimagine ourselves as courageous actors capable of achieving transformative change *now*.

How to Read These Pages: Who, What, and Why

We offer these pages as an introductory guide for beginners in the field of contemplative inquiry and holistic education to better understand the crisis of imbalance we find ourselves in today, as well as for seasoned educators and researchers interested in exploring a narrative approach to the crisis. Our goal is not to overturn every rock, or introduce every essential piece of scholarship, but to take you on an engaging journey that activates your whole being—mind, body, heart, and spirit—ultimately inspiring you to join us on a journey of *restorying for change*.

Because *restorying* is a creative process requiring personal investment and openness to new narrative beginnings, we have attempted to create a structure for our book which will, as much as possible, transport you to a safe and comfortable space, preferably one you associate with stories—perhaps that is your childhood bed, listening to your parents read; or the warmth of a campfire, with marshmallows and flashlights; or the comfort of your favorite reading chair, with something comforting to drink. To reinforce this, we have contextualized the academic concepts of each chapter in personal stories (Amanda and Jing's) and organized the material into "Acts" and "Scenes," rather than Chapters and Sub-Chapters, and even included a storytelling interlude half-way through, which we hope will serve as a calming narrative break. If we are lucky, these choices will sprinkle a handful of magic dust on your reading experience, helping it to recall the feeling of being told a good story on a cool summer evening, one that captures your attention and pulls you in both personally and emotionally.

A Note on Inspiration and Structure

A Dialogue

This book began as a written conversation between the authors, Amanda and Jing, in the Fall of 2019. Amanda was a doctoral student at the University of Maryland at the time, but due to personal and professional circumstances, she was living in Beijing. Despite Amanda's location, Jing offered her the opportunity to engage in the Ecological Ethics and Education seminar she was offering that Fall. In lieu of attending class in person, where she would have been participating in course discussions and activities, Amanda agreed to write a reflection paper each week on the readings.

Amanda was deeply inspired by the articles, stories, and videos curated by Jing for the class, and so these weekly papers quickly became mini essays. Because she was in Beijing at the time, these reflections often include sights and experiences of living in China. Jing responded to Amanda's essays each week, adding thoughtful comments and pushing her to consider the issues more deeply. This back-and-forth created a dialogue over core elements of climate change and education that could have ended there—a series of thoughtful essays and responses saved on our respective computers—but Jing, a contemplative educator committed to empowering her students, saw the conversation as a beginning rather than an end, and suggested that we reformulate our essays and responses into the book you are holding today.

Jing's approach was (and is) an example of non-traditional education in that it allowed for a co-creation between teacher and student that sidestepped the hierarchy of teacher *over* student, a traditional mode of education, which still forms the basis of many classrooms today. In the spirit of co-creation, we have chosen to retain the original structure of a dialogue to emphasize what is possible when a teacher not only treats her students as intellectual equals but also goes out of her way to approach their ideas with respect, curiosity, and openness. We believe that the spirit of co-creation that began back in 2019 runs through these pages and we encourage you to consider it as one of the book's many offerings.

Because Amanda's essays, which rely heavily on personal narration, were the first to put the powerful resources of Jing's course into writing, Amanda is the main narrator. She writes about her journey with Jing's course in first person, referencing many of the assigned readings, along with articles and papers she discovered along the way. But it was the collected readings of Jing's course, fastened into a sixteen-week journey for her students over many years, which serve as both bedrock and stream for Amanda's reflections. As such, Jing's spirit is like a guiding force, having inspired each chapter. Her first-person experiences, insights, and stories are also interwoven through the book as responses to Amanda's writing, designed to help us all reflect more deeply on what has been said, and at times consider new ways of thinking and knowing.

Suggested Reflective Activities

In the spirit of dialogue and co-creation, throughout the book we invite you, dear reader, to enter into the conversation and personalize the material through a series of Suggested Reflective Activities. We believe (and researchers agree) that the process of reflection and personalization will deepen your engagement and learning.[1] If done with intention, these activities will simultaneously serve to pull you into a journey of discovery alongside us, so that we can move together through the story of these pages.

While some space is provided for writing, to make the most use of the Suggested Reflective Activities we suggest you read with a journal nearby, or a pen to make notes in the margins and empty spaces. You might also consider reading with a group of like-minded people and sharing or discussing your answers, offering a second layer of learning. But regardless of how you engage with this book, we encourage you to remember that you are not alone. All of us—humans, animals, and plants alike—are in this together.

Table of Contents: A Guide to Restorying in 4 Acts

Act I: *Understanding Where We Are Now*

Before creating something new, first we must understand *where*, and in *what state*, we are starting. Act I explores this question in 3 Scenes:

Scene 1: Setting the Scene: Stories That Have Formed Us Culturally and Personally
Scene 2: Our Connection with the Earth and Love for Nonhumans
Scene 3: The Western Cultural Imaginary: Stories That Taught Us to Value the Mind Over the Body

Act II: *Envisioning and Preparing for the Journey Ahead*

In Act II we sharpen our senses and begin the creative work of inspiring and preparing for the journey of a lifetime, gathering the intellectual, spiritual, and emotional tools we need.

Scene 4: Inspiration: Stories of Vision and Change
Scene 5: Preparation: Tools for Accessing Inner Wisdom and Love

—An Interlude: *Two Stories*—
Here we pause in our journey to tell two stories we hope will bring Acts I and II to life:

The Story of Andrew: An International Businessman
The Story of Amanda's Trip to Phnom Penh, Cambodia

Act III: *From Root to Branch: Considering the Myriad Ways We Learn to Be*

In Act III we turn our attention to education and influences on our learning.

Act IV: "Restorying" for Change: What Does It Mean and How Does It Work?

Here we explore research on the use of storying and *re*-storying to create change, then turn the focus around to you, asking you to name your current story, then **restory** yourself into a courageous actor capable of creating transformative change.

Getting to Know One Another

By means of introducing ourselves, let us share some personal stories . . .

Amanda: I had no idea what to expect from China when I moved there in 2018. I had lived in Wuxi, China, some twenty years before, in 2001, as a naïve and hopeful twenty-something. What I remember are long fields of open space in a long blur through a train window. Unhappy workers with stained uniforms who hardly looked me in the face. Buying bowls of oily vegetables from street stalls. Red Bean popsicles that tasted amazing. People pointing and yelling at me in amazement because of my white skin and foreign face. Rivers of bicycles that were impossible to break.

On my way to China I traveled through Beijing. I visited Tiananmen Square and the Forbidden City. I remember gazing across a completely open, flat slab of grey concrete at the Communist Leader Chairman Mao's face, taking tuk tuks all the way up to the front gates of the Forbidden City. Today, all streets around the Forbidden City and Tiananmen Square have been widened considerably and completely blocked to traffic, while the front gate is accessible only through security check points. The excitement of chaotic streets and colorful markets has been replaced by a highly controlled, anesthetized feeling of a startlingly powerful authoritarian state. No one goes in or out without showing their ID Cards or passports, walking through metal detectors, and having their faces scanned by facial recognition software. The day I returned to Tiananmen Square in 2019 it was closed to foot traffic, and so I stood from the other side of the street taking pictures that look like nothing.

The charm Beijing has lost in the last twenty years has been replaced by the undeniable feeling of power, significance, and luxury. Tuk tuks have been all but replaced by taxi services, which offer any kind of cars you'd like—a regular city taxi with a meter; an "express" car, which is like an Uber; or a "luxury" car with a leather interior and free bottles of water for each seat. Nearby the Forbidden City is the National Center for the Performing Arts, an egg-shaped architectural wonder surrounded by water on all sides. At night the lights of the building periodically shimmer from blue to pink to yellow in a futuristic show that draws photographers and young couples alike.

I quickly learned that Beijing is, in many ways, more technologically advanced than the United States. For example, cash and credit cards have been almost entirely replaced by smart-phone apps like WeChat Pay and Alipay. Even street vendors will display a QR code for you to scan with your phone as this is their preferred method of payment. In my first few weeks I found it difficult to buy anything—a cup of coffee, a meal. It finally sank in that I would need to reassess my approach to payment for good when I went into a Western-themed restaurant to buy dinner and tried to pay with my international credit card (which I have used in a dozen foreign countries) only to be met with sincere regret at not being able to serve me. It took the restaurant manager nearly ten minutes of rustling around in the back to unearth an old credit-card machine that was, thank God, able to read my old technology. In less foreigner-friendly places, however, shop owners would simply smile and shake their heads, completely unable to accommodate me. The smaller the store, the harder this would be. For a traveler passing through, who does not just stick to the international hotels and bars that cater to them, Beijing's technological advancement can be crippling. Once you have

adjusted, however, the possibilities quickly become astounding.
My personal favorite are the vending machines. These have QR
codes which, when scanned, cause the machine's menu to pop
up on your phone, allowing you to choose an item and pay, all
without having to touch a button on the machine!

If you stay in Beijing long enough, you will come to realize
that anything—really, anything—can be delivered. A cup of
coffee, a finger-cake, a screwdriver, a box of get-well cookies
that you made and want to send to a sick friend on the other
side of the city (the city is huge, encompassing 6,336 square
miles with over 21 million inhabitants). The army of delivery
men who spend all day on their scooters running items back
and forth feel, after a while, like a kind of extended family. I
felt obligated to open doors for them, give directions, and run
out to meet them when they had trouble finding me. They have
hot/cold bags on the backs of their bikes and an app on their
phone that operates like Uber Eats—when a delivery order is
made, the first to accept it rushes to the chosen location while
the customer watches their progress digitally. All over the
city you can see them zipping through the streets, waiting at
restaurants for orders, running through apartment complexes
and office buildings. My students often had one singular cup of
coffee delivered to our office followed by, a few minutes later, a
sandwich—anything they wanted, anywhere, at any time, and
cheap. Nearly everyone I knew ordered out multiple times a day.
It was a convenience unparalleled in the United States, and it
would have been something to love and marvel at if it were not
for the endless mounds of single-use containers in tied-up plastic
bags overflowing from garbage cans in every neighborhood.

I worked at Greenpeace for three years in my late twenties.
It was there that I began, in earnest, my education on the life
cycle of consumer products and the urgency of the climate
crisis, but it wasn't until I lived in Beijing that I began to truly
understand what is on the line. At least fifty percent of the time I
woke up to a smog-choked sky and warnings about "hazardous"
or "very unhealthy" air quality. I bought two large HEPA air
filter machines for my little apartment and ran them every day.
Pre-Covid, I was already keeping an array of masks by the front
door and stashed in coat pockets; sometimes even these weren't
enough to save me from the headaches.

Seeing a sliver of blue overhead, or rays of sun through
clouds, was a rare and precious thing. For long-term Beijingers,

the pollution of 2018–20 is nothing; they went through much worse ten years ago and count themselves lucky. But I, coming from a place with wide blue skies and visible sunsets, quickly began to long for the blue of the sky, and feel the loss of this taken-for-granted beauty in my body. The grey skyscape made for a surreal backdrop to the colorful storefronts that decorate Beijing's streets, and the coordinated light shows that dance up and down its buildings. I quickly learned that no amount of art or colorful light displays can make up for not seeing the sun or stars on a regular basis. Even a wander through the hutongs—a collection of traditional neighborhoods in Beijing that have retained the original architecture of narrow alleys, stout concrete buildings, tiled roofs, and communal living, all of which make you feel as if you are stepping back in time—couldn't cancel out the frustrations of being afflicted with a sore throat after finally giving in and taking a walk despite air quality warnings.

Jing: I grew up in China, on a state-owned farm in the 1960s and 1970s. At that time, we could be said to live a poor life, as there was no excess of any material goods, but the sky was extremely blue, sparrows were everywhere, and you could catch fish with your bare hands. Often, it was so quiet from a lack of cars or motorcycle sounds that it seemed eerie. Parents allowed their children to roam around as there were no traffic accidents to worry about. Daily, we lived among the sounds of crowing roosters, barking dogs, and loud singing frogs. Often, I followed my family's turkey to the deep grass where she laid her eggs, and I picked wildflowers as my trophies.

As a little girl, I once spent hours pouring water into a small hole until a small insect climbed out of it and pooped on my hand! We told stories of ghosts and got excited about movies that were always played in the open, with a piece of white cloth as the screen hung between two poles or trees. Our family of seven people (my parents, four children, and my grandma) lived on a total income of 70 yuan per month (about $10 today). Life was hard, no food was wasted, and very little trash was produced. Scary stories told by my grandmother were our entertainment before we went to bed.

After I graduated from high school, I left the state farm and moved to the provincial capital city—where there were no high-rise buildings—to attend college. With economic reform and market liberalization sanctioned by the government under the leadership of Deng Xiaoping, streets started to be filled with merchants selling all kinds of goods. Folks who made money were established as role models, and people started to be bombarded with the message that time is money, and speed is money. The whole province, in fact, the whole country began on a path of chasing GDP growth and the accumulation of wealth— what Amanda described became a reality all over the country. Even the remotest part of the country has choking smoke, and everywhere you go, mountains and valleys are being turned into real estate development sites. A huge river behind my grandparents' house totally dried up and disappeared . . .

Amanda: There are parts of Beijing that are so dry, the entire landscape looks like cracked earth. Dirt seems starved into sand, the trees sickly. Unsurprisingly, perhaps, water is undrinkable from the tap, which means you must buy bottled water or have filters installed and changed regularly. After a few months of showering I realized my hair was breaking off and my skin was itchy because of the heavy mineral deposits I was being exposed to every time I took a shower. Many foreigners, myself included, eventually have filters installed in the shower heads. This struggle for fresh, clean water and healthy skin is part and parcel of living in Beijing, but Beijing is by no means unique.

According to the CDC (2019), China is joined by at least 187 other countries whose tap water is undrinkable, including Taiwan, Vietnam, Cambodia, Indonesia, India, South Africa, Turkey, Morocco, Chad, Brazil, Argentina, and Mexico (we should add that this is also true, of course, in some parts of the United States).[2] Like many people around the world, in order to live and be healthy Beijingers are forced to become complicit in one of the many unsustainable practices that is directly contributing to the climate crisis: the continual purchase, and disposal, of water in plastic bottles.

This point was driven home for me one wintry afternoon as I sat at my desk on the second floor of my apartment in Shunyi. I was reading the words of Patricia Mische (1991), who reminded me that "Earth is a water planet. It is, in fact, over two thirds water," and "we are water beings, comprised of two thirds water and requiring fresh water daily to survive," when I was alerted by a knock on the door to my monthly water delivery.[3]

With Mische's words ringing in my mind, I dragged four cardboard boxes into my apartment, each with four one-gallon plastic bottles of water inside. This would keep me drinking coffee, water, and making soup for the next month at least. I had to buy and throw each of those bottles away or be sick. This regretful, depressing reality is a regular practice for many around the world who don't have access to clean water any other way. As the climate disaster worsens, of course, and resources are depleted, water will become even more expensive and scarce, eventually turning even this seemingly wasteful act into a luxury. According to UNICEF (2022), "almost two thirds of the world's population" struggles with "severe water scarcity for at least one month each year," and that this could be extended to half of the world's population by as early as 2025.

Even in places where tap water is clean, we still have to buy vegetables and meat wrapped in plastic and affixed to plastic or Styrofoam trays; use cars fueled by gasoline to drive to the store; and use stoves powered by coal to do our cooking. Every day we are complicit in a series of small destructive actions which it is hard to find a way around making. Aside from living off the grid and hunting our own food each day, we are largely beholden to an industrialized food, water, and transportation system that is destroying our planet. These small, daily actions force us into a conundrum of conscience, a state which living in Beijing forced me into more viscerally each and every day. Surprisingly, however, it seemed as if I was in the minority of people in China who felt this way.

In general, the Chinese people didn't seem to think at all about the waste we were producing. People were in love with their to-go lifestyle, just as we are in the United States, and honestly, it was hard not to get caught up in the convenience of it, even for someone who cares deeply about the climate, like me. My friends and students may have complained about the pollution, but they were clearly happy about the strong economy—nobody seemed interested in sacrificing the economic advances they'd made for a clear blue sky. In this way China joins a slew of countries around the world for whom destruction of the environment and its concomitant effect on people's health is understood as "an acceptable price for economic progress" (Klein, 2014, p. 19). They are proud of their well-run subway system that connects the city to surrounding areas, and they are happy about their growing presence on the world stage, and why shouldn't they be? The United States and much of the Western world have been carelessly building their economic strength at the expense of the environment for centuries.

Jing: I remember in the first few years of 2000, I visited China every
year, and each time I thought I was in a new country: I could
not recognize the city or town I had visited the previous year
or even half a year before. Whole cities were pulled down for
total reconstruction, and lakes were filled up for high-priced
apartment buildings and luxury homes. Rivers disappeared
as the environment changed. In a conversation, a government
official shared that it was "necessary" for China to sacrifice the
environment in order to surpass the United States and become
the world's next superpower. The United States and Brittan were
cited as examples of countries that polluted first, in order to
become wealthy and powerful, then they treated the pollution.

Amanda: It was in this Chinese context that I wrote the essays that
would become these pages. They came as I sat in my office in
Shunyi, Beijing, watching my students order cups of coffee and
sweet cakes and hamburgers to ease the difficulty of their studies.
As I walked by the armies of scooters that manned the to-go
apps that everyone used each day. As I passed the overflowing
dumpsters and trash cans and discarded food boxes that littered
the streets. As I donned my mask on bad-air days and looked
forlornly from my apartment window at the smog choking the city.

Jing: What Amanda described is something we touched on in
the class while she was taking it remotely, and I was teaching it
in-person back in the United States: What does "development"
mean? What are the missing parts of "development" that are so
fundamental, such as spiritual development, and the development
of ecological intelligence, through which we become able to feel
and sense the suffering of nature? How have we killed the children
of Mother Nature in our eagerness to "develop"? How have we
been choking her with all our poisonous emissions? What stories
have been told and reinforced that have numbed the nerves and
hearts of both young and old, making this destruction not only
possible, but also lauded as a necessary step "up" the imagined
ladder of economic and societal development?

Introducing "Restorying"

What Story Are You Living Right Now, In This Very Instant?

I, Amanda, am sitting in front of an open window in Taipei (in 2023),
writing on my computer. It is a Frida y night in summer and, like

many summer nights in Taipei, it has just rained, leaving a refreshing gleam across the city. Swinging headlights of scooters create rainbows in the puddles and the air itself seems to exhale from the release. It is a beautiful night to be just where I am, overlooking the narrow alley that leads to the bustling night market that is my neighborhood, writing about the power of stories and the crisis of climate change. In this moment—through the experience of thinking, writing, and being—I am *living and telling* multiple interconnected stories about who I am: stories about myself as a writer, a researcher, a traveler, and a woman who cares about climate change.

If I were to ask where these stories that characterize myself as a writer and a thinker began, I would have to travel all the way back to childhood to find my answer. Back to the quiet girl with the flourishing inner world who always felt out of sync and out of place with strangers. To cope with feelings of estrangement I became a voracious reader. The stories I read were a powerful and consistent escape, teaching me to respect and adore the written word at a young age. Before long, reading morphed into writing—reading offered a glimpse of a different world, while writing offered a tool for *doing something* with my feelings. Getting them down physically onto a page was a release; organizing these feelings into stories and poems was a way to process and transform even my most difficult experiences into something meaningful . . . beautiful, even.

My relationship with the power of the written word has followed and supported me through every stage of my life, from childhood to the story I am living and telling today: that of a PhD Candidate conducting dissertation research in Taipei, editing this book about the power of stories. Every move I've made and every subject I've approached as an academic has been affected by this story—from the deeply personal moments of sharing my writing with friends as a teenager, to the groups I have joined and the community programming I created, to the Masters of Fine Arts (MFA) I pursued in fiction, and the years I spent as a lecturer in academic writing departments . . . even the way I responded to the first course I took at the University of Maryland with Dr. Jing Lin (co-author of these pages), which led me to redesign my academic writing course around students' stories. It should be no surprise that as a researcher, my inclination has been to seek out methodologies that centralize the collecting of people's stories. It seems that every step I took has its roots in my most sacred childhood narrative, the one I have been internally narrating since I first picked up a pen and wrote my feelings in a diary.

Without the interconnected web of story and experience that form my life I would not be in this exact time or place: I would not be considering the crisis of the climate through the lens of story, nor writing an introduction through the medium of story. In fact, I very likely would not have responded to Dr. Jing Lin's course on Ecological Ethics in 2019 with the series of personal essays that inspired us to write these pages, positing **(re)storying** as a tool for combatting the overwhelming, even paralyzing, crisis of the climate. As such, the stories I have been living and telling since childhood continue to form and shape my life, including the very story I am living and telling today.

Similarly, I (Jing), am sitting here today, writing this introduction to a book about Restorying Our Relationship with Nature. I grew up in China and went to the United States in the mid-1980s to seek knowledge, and after landing an academic job in Canada, I encountered Eastern meditation practice, which all of a sudden, opened me up to feeling the life force and spirits of all things and beings including nature. I started to feel acutely that Mother Nature is alive, and that we are all interconnected. With this new awareness, I want to do something when I read devastating news about climate change, species extinction, and destruction of nature. I started to explore the causes leading to the destructions and hoped that I could do something to raise people's awareness. This led to the creation of the course on Ecological Ethics and Education, which Amanda took with me, and which resulted in the writing of this book.

What is your story?

Pause for a moment and ask yourself—in this moment, right now, as I read the introduction to a book entitled *Storying Our Relationship with Nature*—what stories am I **living and telling about who I am**?

> Maybe you're telling stories about being . . .
> An *academic*
> An *educator*
> A *student*
> An *environmental activist*
> A *parent*

These stories may be deeply ingrained, and so it may require some reflection to bring them into your conscious mind.

If it feels right, take a deep breath in. As you breathe out, let yourself sink into this moment with an awareness of where you are and what you are doing. Perhaps even let the pages blur for a moment and let *yourself* come into focus, then ask the question again—what does it mean about who I am that I am here, *right here, right now*, sitting, standing, leaning over a table with my fingers splayed, reading this introduction?

Suggested Reflective Activity #1: Your Story

In this very instant, what story are you telling?

In the Reflective Activity that follows you will be guided through a 4-step process for reflecting on and better understanding the stories you live and tell every day. For each question posed, your goal is to notice what comes up, and capture those feelings through FREE WRITING. As you write, try not to edit or overthink. Simply let your thoughts arise and flow onto the page, then read them over with an open mind . . .

We invite you to FREE WRITE on any or all of the following questions:

PART A: Articulating Your Story

1. What stories are you living and telling *right now?*
   Specifically focus on stories that help you to understand who you are, and how you got to where you are today.
2. How do these stories connect to stories that began in childhood? That is, stories about your family, friends, hometown, or who you were as a child?

PART B: What Forms Our Stories

Consider that ever since the first prince and princess were called forth in our minds, painted into an idealized kingdom which existed *a long, long time ago, in a land far, far away*, we have experienced the power of setting; our personal stories are no different. Each of them begins with a particular time and place, decked out from top to bottom in an inner landscape of personal experiences and beliefs. This inner landscape—where we are *intellectually, emotionally, and spiritually*—determines the way we understand the world around us and influences the choices we make; in other words, our life stories are deeply informed by the beliefs we carry.

Do you believe in God?

Do you believe the universe has a vibrating field of interconnected energy?

Do you believe the Earth, and all its creatures, have a right to life?

Do you believe that you are *powerful and courageous enough* to create meaningful change?

1) What are three (or more) beliefs I carry about:

    a.   myself
    b.   the Earth
    c.   my ability to create change

2) What other (if any) major beliefs do I carry?

PART C: Tone and Tenor of Our Stories

Together with your belief systems is your outlook: the tone and tenor of your stories. For example, if we (Amanda and Jing) did not approach our personal stories about the power of individual humans in the climate crisis with an *empowering and determined tone*, we would not have taken the time to write this book, let alone have the boldness to assume it was worthy of being read by other people. In this way, it is the *tone and tenor* of our stories that *determines their narrative arc* and opens us up to a particular world of possibility.

3) What is the *tone and tenor* of *my* story? That is, what do I
    believe I am capable of accomplishing?

PART D: Assessing Our Stories

If the beliefs we hold, and/or the actions we take, don't honor those we love, or serve our vision of a better world, then it is time for change.

To delve deeper, FREE WRITE on the following:

1) Do my *actions* match my beliefs?

    a.   If so, in what way?
    b.   If not, why?

2) Are the stories I'm living and telling helping me to shape the world I most want for myself and future generations?

    a.   If yes, in what way?
    b.   If not, why not? What needs to change?

Act I

UNDERSTANDING WHERE WE ARE NOW

Scene 1

SETTING THE SCENE

STORIES THAT HAVE FORMED US
CULTURALLY AND PERSONALLY

The stories we have shared seem despairing. Indeed, we have reason to feel that way. Most of us know we are living beyond our means, and by and large, our international institutions agree. The U.N. General Assembly (2019) says that we have less than eleven years to "prevent irreversible damage" and the U.N. declared climate change as "the defining issue of our time," making this moment, right now, a "defining moment."[1] Tom Rivett-Carnac, expert in climate policy and lobbyist for the UN, reminds us that unlike pandemics and social unrest, which may feel never-ending while we're in them, "the climate crisis will be permanent."[2] As sea ice melts, it not only raises sea levels, but also affects the way heat is distributed around the planet, which will, in turn, lead to droughts, unprecedented monsoons, and the collapse of ecosystems, ultimately shifting the planet into an entirely new climate to which humans will not be suited.[3] In other words, our planet will slip out of balance with human beings. It will flip from a climate system that supports and nourishes us to a system of chaotic weather and extremes that will threaten our lives and homes on a regular basis. Until balance is rediscovered—if that is even possible—we will be at its mercy.

Around the world, natural disasters caused by climate change are rising. Although exact numbers vary widely, the World Health Organization notes that "[g]lobally, the number of reported weather-related natural disasters has more than tripled since the 1960s" and "every year, these disasters result in over 60,000 deaths, mainly in developing countries."[4] The unprecedented 2022 monsoon season in Pakistan is a devastating example—the rainfall was at least five times higher than normal across the country, affected 30 million people, and killed more than 1,000.[5] In an emergency call for aid to be given to Pakistan, UN Chief Antonio Guterres called out Southeast Asia as a hot spot, saying people are "15 times more likely to die from climate impacts" if they live in that region.[6]

While a flood of the size of what Pakistan saw in 2022 would be devastating anywhere, the infrastructure of less developed countries makes poor citizens, with less resources and options, especially vulnerable.[7] According to the International Disaster Database, the highest death tolls in 2019 occurred in countries such as India, Mozambique, Zimbabwe, Indonesia, Bangladesh, Nepal, Myanmar, and China, where infrastructure and disaster response systems are less capable than those of their more developed trade partners.[8] Equally vulnerable, or perhaps even more vulnerable, is the ecosystem itself, including animals, plants, and even insects, which depend on a healthy environment for their survival.

Unfortunately, as Naomi Klein put it in 2014, "what the climate needs to avoid collapse is a contraction in humanity's use of resources" while "what our economic model demands to avoid collapse is unfettered expansion," a bleak truth that puts us in an extremely difficult situation.[9] But no matter how difficult it might seem, the truth is that something will have to give at some point, and as Naomi Klein intoned, it won't be the laws of nature. If we want to avoid the collapse of our planet, we will need to find a way to rediscover and ultimately preserve the balance we once had with Mother Nature.

When we look at climate change as a crisis of balance, and when we consider the Earth not as something separate or apart, but a system in which we are all integrated, then the high levels of CO2 in the air, plastics in the oceans, and toxins in the soil all become symptoms of an internal sickness—*we are out of balance with ourselves, and as a result we are pushing the Earth further out of balance with human beings.*

The good news is that it does seem, at long last, that people are beginning to listen. In the Climate Summit of 2022 (COP 27), a long-awaited agreement was signed in which rich nations agreed to provide financial support for less developed nations struggling to cope with natural disasters.[10] The European Union is making enormous strides in its shift to renewable energy, finalizing plans to achieve a net reduction of 55 percent of greenhouse gas emissions by 2030.[11] And the United States, which as of the writing of this book is back in the Paris Climate Accords, made net zero carbon emissions the goal for 2050. The United States Congress also passed the Inflation Reduction Act, which is the first substantial climate change legislation for the United States in its history. Within this historical piece of legislation, however, are incentives to develop and use Carbon Capture and Sequestration

(CCS) technology, which many climate activists argue is nothing more than a band-aid solution, allowing the coal industry to continue with business as usual by "capturing" their emissions and storing them underground. The coal industry, along with other big polluters affected by climate change legislation, have been lauding CCS as a solution for decades while environmentalists have been pushing back based on the facts as we know them. First, CCS requires the investment in more infrastructure and energy to build and run, not less, and past projects have continually increased emissions.[12] Second, CCS is expensive and paid for with public funds, yet not proven to be more effective than renewable energy solutions, with approximately 80 percent of CCS projects to date having ended in failure.[13] Despite the perceived promises of CCS—namely, that we could continue using coal—it remains unproven, unstable, and a distraction from the changes to lifestyle and infrastructure that addressing the crisis of climate change requires. That it continues to appear in every climate change bill and discussion is evidence of the complexity of the problem we face when it comes to making transformative change in our energy infrastructure.

Concessions to and compromises with big polluters are nothing new, of course; these industries have successfully integrated themselves into every part of our modern society, from daily living to the halls of Congress. Our most promising avenues for rising to the challenge of climate change are consistently guided by companies like Shell, BP, and Chevron, who were even invited to sponsor the U.N. Climate Summit of 2019 while simultaneously investing more than $50 billion in projects that "will not be economically viable if governments implement the Paris Agreement on climate change."[14] These facts underscore the complexity of our situation, and highlight one of the main arguments of this book: to create meaningful change in the world, we will need an extraordinary amount of courage, imagination, and determination. We need the *courage* to stand up to multinational companies which have deeply integrated themselves into our lives, the *imagination* to believe in a different way of living, and the *determination* to push past roadblocks that will arise, staying the course despite its difficulties. As we said in our introduction, the science is unequivocally in agreement and widely dispersed, so it seems clear that what is missing is not more evidence, but, rather, an *inner* change that will help human beings to hear the information differently.

We (Amanda and Jing) posit that the necessary change will be one that leads to an understanding of the natural world as an interconnected ecosystem of life in which we are inextricably intertwined (rather than something separate, or external), thereby rendering the continued destruction of our planet emotionally and spiritually intolerable.

Jing: While reading Amanda's writing, I was reminded of a recent trauma right on campus where I teach: the university has just cut down many huge trees in order to build more dormitories and a new metro line on campus. The huge trees had been standing there for decades, but now their severed trunks are scattered around. It was traumatic for me to see them cut down after appreciating and loving them for nearly two decades. They were not just beautiful, or givers of shade, but citizens and teachers to our campus community. I mourned the loss of those trees and later organized a workshop to talk about trees, including my deeply felt belief that they are our teachers and elders, guarding students, faculty, and staff, providing life support to all of us. Of course, they were also homes to birds and squirrels and many other nonhumans whom we never consider as relevant while making decisions to cut down trees—as if the lives of non-humans are inconsequential. The trees were treated as objects/obstacles to be removed at our convenience, without a second thought. At the same time, there was a discussion to make the golf course next to the campus a huge parking lot because the university has joined the Big Ten and thousands of visitors will flock to the campus for games. As I watch more and more green space being turned into concrete, and more and more of our nonhuman family members callously destroyed, I feel the disconnect between ourselves and the natural world as a kind of illness that is leading to so much trauma, which so many of us do not take the time to consider or understand.

Beijing Stories

I am writing this after a two-day stretch of walking back and forth to my Beijing office despite a depressing air quality reading of over 250 ppm, which turns the skies gray and actually results in a mist-like cloud constantly hovering in the distance. On such days I wear a mask everywhere I go and blast my industrial-sized air filter, which I can only pray works properly. People who have lived in Beijing for years laugh when I tell them I think it's a "bad-air day." They have learned to live with the pollution the way some people back home have to learn to live with long commutes or difficulty parking. My students tell me that one year it reached 1000 ppm, so to them 200 or 250 is no big deal. My friends who have children at the international schools tell me that as long as it's 150 or below, the children are allowed outside to play. For comparison's sake, I once, in a fit of frustration and cabin fever, rode my bike for two hours in 140 ppm and afterwards my throat felt raw for three days. Once one of my students pulled out a screen shot he had taken in November of 2018 that showed readings of between 500 and 1000 ppm across the city; he showed it almost proudly, as if he was proving something to me rather than revisiting a regretful, horrid memory. But humans are adaptable beings, and so perhaps those who have lived with pollution all their lives just don't take it very seriously—I worry that this ability we have to continue with our lives, to ignore and push aside without the attention of mindful thinking, will be the death of us one day.

For now, as a foreigner in this place, I walk around with a mask on in 250 ppm and my scarf wrapped around my face on top of that, but I hardly see anyone else doing the same. I see people on dates, children running through our community park, families meandering around the shopping mall where I have my office. The threat seems falsely diminished when I look at how the people living in it, day in and day out, adapt so fully. Of course, air pollution isn't nearly as alarming as typhoons or nuclear disasters or hurricanes; it doesn't kill us on contact, but slowly, over time.

> **Jing**: Concomitantly, I was teaching about these same air pollution issues in class. I showed the students images of blackened skies, so dark in China in some years in winter that you could hardly see a few feet away from you. People did their business in darkness; sometimes it was so dark that schools were cancelled, and public buses stopped running. I also showed similar images of cities in Pakistan, India, and many other countries of the world.
>
> **Amanda**: It is amazing how sheltered we are from air pollution in the United States, yet how much of the Earth is suffering. It is also frightening to think about how adaptable we are as human beings—will we simply adjust as the Earth cracks apart around us? How far will we let it go before we are moved to change?

Environmental Stories

My introduction to the environmental movement came through three years of working with the US branch of the international environmental non-profit Greenpeace (GP). I was the Administrative Assistant to the Actions Team in Washington DC from 2006 to 2009, but in this role, I was given the opportunity to do much more than answering phones and booking travel for my team. I learned how to design and coordinate direct actions which shut down coal conferences, hung banners off buildings and bridges, projected images in all kinds of unexpected places, and helped organize mass marches through city streets to raise awareness for the climate. Toward the end of my three years with GP, I chose to partake in several actions that risked arrest and was subsequently arrested twice—once for trespassing on the private property of a Coal Plant, and once for hanging a banner off a bridge in San Francisco.

Throughout those three years I was immersed in a group of some of the smartest and passionate people I had ever met, all of them dedicating their lives to the environmental movement (despite its low salary when compared to the private sector). Many of them were willing to put their lives on the line for what they believed, and to spend multiple nights in jail without batting an eye. Looking back on those people and that time, I think that for them—and for me—a deep, loving relationship with nature was a given. We went camping and out on boats as regular group practice. We gathered around campfires and stared in awe at the stars. When we were out on an assignment, we always took the time to find a hot spring or a natural park and gaze at the beauty around us in wonder and appreciation.

Another thing I am grateful to have experienced through my time at GP was the complex look at the variety of opinions that existed in the world. We had a front row seat to the powerful wall of government officials, industry leaders, and—most disturbing of all—average citizens who disregarded our passion as annoying and naïve. Many thought we were crazy hippies with nothing better to do than to disrupt traffic or ask for money while they were trying to get to work, and told us so at every opportunity. But in the midst of some of the more disappointing interactions we had, there was also the opening of doors that before had been shut, and slivers of possibility that revealed themselves in the most unlikely of places.

One of the actions I helped coordinate involved delivering a message to coal executives at a coal conference. We had spent nearly three months preparing to clandestinely infiltrate the group, and in preparation we had purchased a table outside of the conference under a different name where we planned to launch a series of small protests: a small group of kids, who had gotten asthma due to living near a coal plant, would be passing out asthma inhalers with messages on them; and one of our directors, who was particularly well spoken, was planning to take over the microphone and give a speech. On our table we planned to set out glass jars of water from a river in North Carolina which had been so badly polluted by a coal plant that people could no longer bath in it, let alone drink from it. We also had videos and pictures of mountain-top removal sites and packets of information, including a well-researched report on the human and environmental costs of coal. At the very last minute, one of our new hires used a Greenpeace phone to call the conference staff; she left a message, and when they called her back, they got a pre-recorded voice mail from Greenpeace, and suddenly realized who we were.

To our surprise, the conference organizers welcomed us to set up our table anyway, and the coal executives invited us in to give a twenty-minute speech to their captivated audience so that we did not need to interrupt the conference to send our message. After the speech was given the conference broke for lunch. I was standing behind our table in the hallway when a tall man in a crisp black suit stopped to talk. He was a climate denier, but he was eager and willing to engage, so I listened to his argument. After going back and forth with him on the reliability of climate change predictions for quite some time, I finally said: "Look, even if it's only just *possible* that the world will one day be unsafe for humans, isn't that scary enough?" And he immediately said, without a hint of sarcasm, "yes." He nodded his head at me then, admitting that I had made my point. Then he shook my hand and walked away. I wonder about him often—if he continued to work in the coal industry despite the sliver of possibility that existed in his heart, or if he brought up our conversation to other people. Regardless, I felt I had accomplished something that day.

> **Jing**: We as a species are largely in a slump. We observe things happening to others or around the world and secretly hope they do not happen to us. Even if things happen to us locally, we choose to neglect the pattern and tell ourselves this is a temporary, one-time thing. I must admit I was in such a state until I started to do meditation and got awakened to the ecological catastrophe we are in. Meditation practice opened up my sensory system and I began to resonate with natural forces and spirits of other species on Earth. I had dreams of standing on a high hill and water was filling up the valley submerging houses down there; I dreamed of flowing in a river full of trash

and it flowed underground still full of trash and into the ocean;
I dreamed of skies becoming dark and humans screaming for
help. Dreams are altered states of consciousness and reveal to us
what could happen; I became much more sensitive since starting
to meditate and became aware of signs of warning everywhere.
I came to the realization that we need to look inward to find
solutions in our world. We are part of nature and nature is
sending us messages that she is suffering. We need to hear her
message in our heart and spirit in order to wake up.

Cultural Stories About What Is Valuable

Economic Stories

Much of our imbalance with Nature seems to be rooted in the story we
tell ourselves about the importance of economic power and individual
wealth. Today, the economic structure of our global society depends on
the flow of money globally—the buying and selling of products created
by industrialists and creative thinkers (supply) and the perceived needs
of consumers (demand). By and large, the value of products bought and
sold has been determined solely by what people are willing to pay for
them while the *impact* of these products, from their creation to their
disposal, has for the most part not been considered. The story we tell
ourselves about the value of money and the importance of a free-market
economy is a well-established one, which has captivated policymakers
and businesspeople for centuries. In trying to better understand our
economic story, in which so much of our cultural understanding of the
marketplace is rooted, Adam Smith is a thinker worth discussing.

Adam Smith, the famed philosopher and economist, is largely
heralded as the "Father of Capitalism." He told a compelling story in
1776 about how pursuing our own, rational selfish interest and allowing
for competition between businesses to satisfy our needs could lead
to prosperity. He argued, in his 1776 treatise *The Wealth of Nations*,
that only by attending to one's "own security" and by directing one's
"industry in such a manner [so that its] produce may be of the greatest
value," will a man do all he needs to do to enrich society.[15]

Smith believed that an economic system set up to monetarily
and socially reward those who designed products well suited for a
blossoming society would guarantee us the best possible society.
To be sure, his vision makes sense on paper. Those visionaries and

creatives with the will and determination to design products will be motivated to design things that people need—because what is needed will sell—for the personal reward of wealth accumulation and status. With the possibility to astronomically increase their station in life, the determination and creativity of this class of people would only increase, and so too would the benefits for society. In this way, Smith envisioned a market-based system where the needs of the majority were taken care of by the selfish instincts of the savvy designers and businessmen of the world. He saw their selfishness—their desire for wealth—as a powerful, positive force that we as a global society could capitalize on intelligently.

In this way, Smith believed that self-interest should be seen as a guiding principle for society. He even went so far as to write, in *The Wealth of Nations*, that "[b]y pursuing his own interest [man] frequently promotes that of society more effectually than when he really intends to promote it." Smith believed that congress people, or those in the employ of the state, could not be trusted to understand what the people might need, and any attempt by them to regulate or otherwise involve themselves in the buying or selling of goods would be pure folly. The implication here is that when local businesspersons acts rationally and in their own interest, they will naturally promote the best interests of society. If this were true, then the society in which we live today, with all of its polluting industries, inequality, weapons production, and penchant for subjugation and violence, would be due to a lack of rational choice. But what is more rational for a consumer than buying the cheapest thing on the market (i.e., cheap, dirty energy)? Or people producing weapons to fill a market demand? Doesn't this make clear the flaws in a system run by pure logic?

Perhaps Smith would argue that our problem isn't the supply and demand that the free markets respond to at will, but, rather, that the markets are not *free enough* due to large governmental subsidies and regulations. For Smith a competitive marketplace *is* a perfect system, allowing all that is good and necessary for society to rise up, and all that is unnecessary or harmful to be phased out by the power of the purse (held by the consumer). This is what is meant by the "invisible hand": it is the invisible hand of the consumer's need cupping our system, making it responsive to society. So, a capitalist society is always responding to the needs of the consumer, which through the power of supply and demand will ensure a well-run society.

What I think Smith overlooked is the nature of selfish interest: when people are motivated by self-interest, they have no incentive to be moral or good in any spiritual or emotional way. In such a system, there is no incentive to value the Earth or human rights. For the true free-market believer, environmental waste and workers' rights will be figured out over time by the market—as it becomes important, consumers will reject products which pollute their air and water, or say no to jobs which exploit or endanger them, and as a result businesses will change their models. This assumes that people always act in their best interest, and that there is no particular urgency to ensure a healthy planet, or equal rights and dignity for all workers.

This story of selfish interest and perfect market-based systems was crafted in 1776; amazingly, it remains deeply ingrained in the global consciousness today. It is passionately argued for on the floor of the United States Congress and demanded on the world stage by international organizations like the World Bank. But let's put aside the economics of Smith's theory and look at the story itself—what is gained through a belief in, or adherence to, this economic narrative? The somewhat cynical answer, perhaps, is that this story justifies the pursuit of self-interest. It gives a logical reasoning for wealth accumulation at all costs, without any thought to the consequences, because it posits a belief in the market as the ultimate arbiter of good and bad. Adherents to Smith's theory feel strongly that if we just leave the market alone, it will eventually take care of the people, because the people are the consumers, and as such choose what perishes and what thrives through the power of their consumer choice. In the world Smith envisioned, and which true free-market capitalists continue to argue for today, we would do away with nearly all government regulations so that the creativity and ingenuity of inventors could be enjoyed by society. In their vision of the world, free-market capitalism will lead to strong economic growth, and in such a world, everyone will benefit. In this story the strength of our GDP is a direct indication of our health as a society.

In the case of Adam Smith's invisible hand, we have inherited a narrative which remains ensconced in the hearts of Western economists and policymakers today. A story believed in by many becomes an ideology, and when enough people act out a story for a long period of time, it becomes ensconced in our very way of living, thinking, and being. But no matter how captivating Adam's Smith story has been, it is not the only possible story.

Tim Jackson, Director of the Centre for the Understanding of Sustainable Prosperity (CUSP), argues that instead of GDP, which relies on "relentless consumption growth and expanding material output," we should develop "a new macroeconomics for sustainability."[16] In the economy he envisions, *investment in the future* would be a key indicator of economic health, as would the *morality* of our markets and fiscal *stability* (rather than growth).[17] If we had the courage and imagination to believe in such a radically different story of what was valuable in our global economy, there's no telling what might be possible!

Development Stories

Deeply intertwined with our story about money and the marketplace is our story about "development" as an ongoing, directional project aimed at moving us from point A to point B. Our development story is rooted in another story—a historically derived *colonial story* of Western superiority—which has captivated an enormous swatch of our global community, teaching them that Christianity, industrialism, and militarism are superior to indigenous belief systems and ways of life. Out of this history has come a largely unquestioned linking of "development" with national economic growth and a centralized nation state. In this way, our story about development has "imposed an economic understanding on social life," leading us to measure the value and success of a nation, its people, and even its culture by the economic standards of one society (the Western one) over all others.

This story of development is so powerful that it has successfully convinced a majority of people around the world to pursue economic development, industrialism, and militarism with a sense of inevitability—as if there is only one possible direction to move in, and only one desirable outcome to imagine. Because so much of this story is rooted in colonialism, it can be helpful to consider the example of at least one story carried by indigenous populations ravaged by colonialism.

An African Indigenous Story[18]

In Africa there is a long history of linking the natural environment with God. Professor and scholar Simon Thurainira Taaliu describes this linking as a belief in "an interconnection of human beings and the natural environment," which warns against exploitation and urges Africans to "take care of the environment so that it can sustain them."[19] Similar to indigenous peoples around the world, Africans lived close to the land and depended on it for their survival prior to colonization. They developed intimate knowledge of the natural world and a spiritual relationship with the Earth and its wonders. This traditional knowledge is described by Taaliu as "a way of life" more than a set of principles; because it was "rooted in the spiritual health, culture, and language of the people," it was seamlessly integrated into choices they made for living wisely, respecting the world's resources, and understanding the need to share. Like other indigenous peoples around the world, the indigenous Africans Taaliu describes view certain lakes, mountains, caves, and trees as sacred, indicating that nature is not "an empty, impersonal object" but an intimate part of life "filled with religious significance."

Before colonialism, education in Africa included the passing down of environmental knowledge and sustainable living practices from one generation to the next through oral tradition, but these elements of traditional African education were largely eradicated by formal colonial schools designed to help the colonial powers exploit the natural resources. These schools trained locals to be clerks, administrators, interpreters, and teachers, and separated people from *the environment as teacher*, placing them in human-focused and productivity-centered classrooms. Over time, the use of technology and the introduction of the market-economy further removed the people from traditional knowledge, disrupting the relationship with nature that had once been so fully integrated. Today, according to the United Nations Conference on Trade and Development (2019), Africa's high-value industries and exports include "petroleum gases; gold; petroleum oils; . . . ; diamonds; and cars," all of which pollute and exploit the environment.[20]

Once people are made dependent for their survival on the buying and selling of goods on the global marketplace, it becomes difficult to raise environmentalism as a central concern. The destruction of a mountain, or the pollution of a clean water supply feels unimportant beside the promise of personal enrichment, or a road map out of poverty. Interrupting this sort of thinking requires a deeper understanding of the links between our own lives and that of the natural world, as well as a transformation of the stories we tell about what is more important: wealth versus health; human beings versus the entire interconnected system. Because of how deeply ingrained these stories are in our cultural imaginary, reimagining them will require the integration of emotion and care into our thinking, and the development of an intimate relationship with the Earth's resources, which quite literally sustain us. Without this shift from a story about the logic of inputs, outputs, and wealth accumulation toward a more balanced story about the interconnection of our lives and our health with that of the Earth, we will continue stumbling recklessly and dangerously toward climate chaos. Sometimes, as this story of African Indigenous thinking makes clear, this transformation is not new at all, but a *returning to* or *a remembering*.

Corporate Stories

I was in Mexico in 2018 when I visited a vegetarian restaurant whose overeager cashier asked if I wanted a to-go container; when I hesitated, he proudly told me that all of their plastics are made from a 100 percent biodegradable material: corn. This is not a perfect solution since it needs very particular composting facilities (not currently common) to be properly processed into "harmless and natural components," and because of ethical concerns involved in turning food into plastics, but it is still a huge improvement over current plastics, which require an estimated 200,000 barrels of oil a day to be made![21] We already know why solutions like these, and research into even better materials, are not being pursued by the plastics industry: the plastics industry alone, as of 2019, was generating over 300 million tons of plastic a year and was valued at more than $4 trillion dollars, which means they have a lot to lose if we were to ever succeed in banning single-use plastics, or forced to undergo any substantial changes to their current infrastructure.[22]

I was recently listening to a news broadcast that caught my attention. Amy Goodman, who is a journalist and host of the independent news organization *Democracy Now!,* was interviewing Sharon Lerner about an in-depth article she had written on the plastics industry for *The Intercept.* They talked about the formation of the non-profit organization, *Keep America Beautiful (KAB),* which is rumored to have been created in response to Vermont's 1953 attempt to create legislation that would require a mandatory deposit, paid at point of purchase, on disposable beverage containers, as well as a ban on the sale of beer in non-refillable bottles. In the same year (1953) organizations like the American Can Company and the Owens-Illinois Glass Company—two companies credited with inventing the disposable can and bottle—and other industry leaders such as Coca-Cola and the Dixie Cup Company, began KAB, which quickly turned into a thriving media organization whose goal was to take control of the narrative about disposable plastic waste before it was demonized irreparably.[23] One thing they did was to create a media campaign that would redirect the public's concern about single plastics away from their *production,* and toward the *disposal by the consumer,* effectively redirecting the responsibility of the plastics waste from the corporations and putting it on the consumer.

One of their most famous and successful ads was a commercial dubbed *The Crying Indian,* which I remember running on TV when I was a teenager, over twenty-five years ago; for me to remember an advertisement so clearly from my youth should be a testament to its impact. I've since looked it up and rewatched it. The descriptive summary that follows is my attempt to capture the content and spirit of the ad:

> A Native American, in a colorful buckskin shirt with a braid over each shoulder, is canoeing purposefully through the still waters of a polluted river to dramatic music. As the music intensifies, the camera zooms out and we see there are polluting factories and plumes of smoke behind him. Finally, he arrives at a sandy bank and sees it littered with plastic. As he beaches his canoe and walks around, looking solemnly disappointed, a voice-over says: "Some people have a deep abiding respect for the natural beauty that was once this country." He walks a little further and we see that the river is just beside a highway. A car drives by and throws a bag of trash out the window, which explodes at the Native American's feet. The voice-over continues, "Some people don't." The Native American looks up, a single tear falling down his face, and the voice-over adds: "People start pollution, people can stop it." The screen then flashes a pamphlet on how you can do your part to change—don't litter, recycle, and so on.

In the narrative presented by *The Crying Indian* ad, the problem of single-use containers was their incorrect disposal (littering) by the consumer *rather than* their production, and therefore their long-term existence in the ecosystem. Their implication was that the problem of plastics in the environment could be solved by thoughtful, consumer-controlled responses, such as recycling, a belief which is still held by many people to this day. This belief in the power of recycling to solve a much deeper problem is an example of a corporate story, used by corporations to divert our attention from the real problem at hand: their existence.

The Crying Indian ad is just one example; you can probably come up with a slew of other corporate stories of your own. These are diversions from the truth that redirect public disapproval from the corporation and toward the consumer, the government, or some other entity—Exxon's use of false climate science to create an alternative narrative around climate change, and Volkswagen's narrative of a low-emission eco-friendly vehicle (while in reality they were cheating on their emissions test because their vehicles would have failed) are two examples.[24,25]

Jing: In the mid-1980s, I came to the United States as an international student. At that time, everyone drank water from the tap, and there was no bottled water. In Michigan, everyone paid 10 cents for beer bottles and Coca-Cola bottles when you checked out and you took the bottles/cans back to the store and got the money refunded. It was a norm, and everyone accepted it. However, the plastics industry started to work with companies selling "natural waters" and gradually created a drinking-from-water-bottle culture, to the point that young people thought it was always like this and do not feel any uneasiness with the huge waste and polluting impact!

Going further back, I remembered when I was little in the 1960s and 1970s. We bought soy sauce, vinegar, sugar, flour, salt . . . by refilling the bottles. In my childhood, my family did not need to change the glass bottle for soy sauce even once. Nowadays, seeing incredibly beautiful glass bottles filled with juice or spaghetti sauce used only once is heartbreaking. We are forced to inadvertently cooperate with the throwaway industry and forced to feel that we have no way out. How sad!

One of the most effective media-manipulation campaigns, propagated by government and big industry, is that environmental change should be done at the individual, consumer level:

- recycle
- buy a hybrid
- turn off your electronics at night
  . . . and all will be well in the ecosystem.

Sure, we should recycle as much as we can, but lately it has become obvious that recycling is **not** a solution to the problem.

First, it is not cost-effective without massive government and tax-payer subsidies, causing many cities and counties around the United States to stop recycling altogether.[26] Second, recycling has been used for generations—as we saw in the *Crying Indian* ad—as a smokescreen for polluting industries. It should be a warning sign that recycling is endorsed by the Plastics Industry Association, a trade group that includes big polluters like Shell, Exxon, Chevron, DowDuPont, and Novolex, all of which profit a great deal from the continued production of plastics. And that the American Recyclable Plastic Bag Alliance—formerly known as the "American Plastic Bag Alliance"—is part of the Plastics Industry Association (a long-time lobbying group that fights against restrictions on plastics) and has long funded promotional and educational efforts around recycling. Why, you might ask? Because as long as there *seems to be* a solution to the problem that doesn't require the industry to slow down production, *they are winning.* This is where the Corporate Narrative comes in.

The American Recyclable Plastic Bag Alliance's narrative attempts to brand themselves as heroes fighting for the environment. They state on their website that they "serve as the frontline defense against plastic bag bans and taxes nationwide," boasting that "standard reusable cotton grocery bags must be reused 131 times to ensure that they have lower global warming potential than a plastic bag used only once," and that "Plastic bags are 100% recyclable and highly reused."[27] This is likely the same logic they use when lobbying to pass legislation aimed at handcuffing local governments in their attempts to ban or restrict single-use plastics. They don't mention that the United States is burning much more of the plastics collected than they are recycling, or that the incineration process releases toxic ash and other pollutants into the air, which are known to cause cancer. And guess where the majority of incinerators are located?

So, sure, in an ideal world we would have a cost-effective, carbon-neutral way to recycle and be able to continue with life as we know it, but since that is NOT currently possible, wouldn't it be a hell of a lot more effective to force the plastics industry to use (and research) biodegradable materials, which will remove this problem altogether? Or force them to return to the culture of reusable bottles that dominated before the plastics industry took off?

Similarly—YES, it is a fantastic idea to reduce our use of electricity and cut down on travel, *but why not force all industries that rely on dirty energy to transform the way they work and invest in renewables in addition*? They are, after all, largely culpable for the problem and benefit a great deal from the continued use of fossil fuels—*why shouldn't they be part of the solution?*

> **Jing:** Money blinds the eyes and hearts of people and corporations. It is heartbreaking to hear that whales and sharks are having loads of plastics (even hundreds of pounds) in their body; it does not even make news that there is a floating island of plastic waste in the Pacific Ocean. Not even the fact that we are literally digesting the equivalent of a plastic credit card every month deters us. We have relied too much on reason, proud that with reason we are a species above other species as articulated by philosophers of the Enlightenment era, but this overemphasis on reason has turned our world into a cold-blooded calculation

of the mind, shutting down our capacity as feeling and empathic beings for the suffering of Mother Nature. How sad that our systems are played with and manipulated to maintain the collective numbness and madness allowing for the destruction of our beautiful home—the Earth.

The Lesson of Cognitive Dissonance

As we have shown in the preceding sections, corporations have consistently avoided responsibility for their actions, even managing to successfully implicate the consumer as culpable for cleaning their mess. However, corporate chicanery does not excuse each of us, *as individuals*, from doing what we can to create positive change. This starts with awareness . . . Consider for a moment all the ways that human beings take part, every single day, in an ecologically, environmentally, and ethically degrading global system.

For example, on my way to Mandarin class today the streets will be clogged with people driving scooters and cars despite Taipei's vast and convenient public transportation system. I will walk by at least ten to-go shops lined innocuously along a busy Taipei street, jammed with customers eager to buy teas, coffees, and assorted snacks packaged in layers of plastic, which will be almost immediately thrown away.

I regularly buy to-go coffees myself, and although I normally bring my reusable to-go cup, I still manage to buy something in a single-use container at least once a week: a bottle of water from 7-11; vegetables from the grocery store displayed on a plastic tray and secured with plastic wrap; even medicines sold in individual plastic pouches. When buying food, I prefer to go to the weekend markets where I can find the same items I would buy in the grocery store, but without the packaging. Yet even here, if I am not quick about it, or feeling lazy that day, the market vendors will put my fruits and vegetables in unnecessary plastic bags which I grudgingly accept and bring home with me. Of course, plastics and gasoline are the obvious culprits—as we discussed in the preceding chapter, there are many less obvious culprits, like where our clothing comes from, or the cost to the environment that exists on our dinner plates. Just walking around our apartments or houses, each one of us could point to a slew of items that are, despite our best intentions, contributing to climate chaos.

While some of us are blissfully unaware of the impact our daily choices make, many more of us are fully aware, yet choose to take a nihilistic or fatalist attitude—namely, there's nothing I can do, so I'm going to just go ahead and live my best life. In this vein of thinking, the buck is passed by individuals back to industry leaders and politicians who are the ones, after all, who have the power to regulate. The problem with this type of thinking is that throughout history it has been shown, again and again, that governments only make inconvenient changes when those changes are turned into a *crisis* by their citizens. For example, slavery wasn't a crisis until abolitionists turned it into one. The rights of women around the world—the right to vote, the right to education, the right to wear what they like and marry whom they wish—was not and will not continue to be a crisis (especially not for the men in power) until women turn it into one. Wars like that which took place in Vietnam, or that which is raging, at the time of this writing, in Ukraine, are considered a crisis only when popular opinion and the vigilance of news agencies consistently and tirelessly insist that it is one. In the same way that, throughout history, discrimination against minorities, immigrants, and displaced people has rarely been treated like a crisis until people demanded it through loud and inconvenient action, so too will the increasing chaos of our planet be downplayed and ignored until a majority of people *demand* it be treated like a crisis. But what needs to change in order for this upsurge of popular disapproval and demand to come?

Many of the biggest corporate polluters have done their own climate research. They have clear ideas of exactly how their products are degrading the environment and either hide the truth of these impacts or launch media campaigns to *change the narrative*. The tendency of the world's biggest polluters to drag their feet on climate legislation despite the risk to their own populations, not to mention populations around the world, seems illogical. Why would anyone choose to set themselves, and the rest of humanity, on such a selfishly destructive path?

Prominent scholar, author, and activist Noami Klein (2014) suggests that the culprit is a state of mind which she labels "cognitive dissonance." Cognitive dissonance refers to the ability to intellectually and emotionally separate our actions from their consequences. She argues we are living in an era of cognitive dissonance, and that taking part in this mass disembodiment is "simply part of being alive in this jarring moment in history, when a crisis we have been studiously ignoring is hitting us in the face—and yet we have been doubling down on the stuff that is causing the crisis in the first place."[28] Perhaps the most interesting takeaway from Klein's insight is the isolation of the problem as a *mental state* rather than a problem of communication, actual solutions, or science. This suggests that the problem runs much deeper than the right government regulations or global climate targets; rather, *it points to the embodiment of a psychological and emotional state* where we see what we want to see, shut out the rest, and plough forward regardless. If the root of the matter is a state of being, feeling, and thinking—rather than an understanding of the science that, let's face it, has reached its likely saturation point with the public—then perhaps we do not need more logic-based solutions. Perhaps more attempts to "educate the public" and "garner support from politicians" is a fool's errand. What we need, it seems, is a change of hearts and minds.

> **Jing**: Many of the efforts we have made remain at the intellectual level, as sound bites made and words written in documents with no living substance. The message of the planet in crisis needs to be felt in the heart and the body of the speakers, listeners, and readers. Ultimately, the question is: Who calls the final shots?! Mother Nature will have the ultimate say! We won't change until we sense the life-force, energy, and spirit of all existence; until we resonate with the will to live of nonhuman beings on earth; see the spirits of mountains and flowers; hear water as the blood flowing in the veins of Mother Nature; and envision oil as her bone marrow, and mountains as her backbone. The tradition that has been overrun by colonialism, industrialism, and capitalism needs to be revived. These are indigenous traditions, Buddhist and Daoist traditions, African animism . . . traditions that say everything has spirit, and all existence is made with the same divine element.

Cultural Stories About Ego and Identity: Who Decides?

I remember in 2000, as an undergraduate student, I took a course on Noam Chomsky with a professor and Chinese scholar, Henry Rosemont. It was in Professor Rosemont's living room, with our classmates sitting in a circle around his coffee table, that he told us something that has remained clear in my mind ever since: *individualism is cultural.* This means that the belief we have in a self that is unique and separate, with distinct rights—an idea that is sacred to us as Westerners—is *particular* to us as Westerners. It is not a universal truth, or something inherent in every human being, but culturally derived.

I remember the shock this caused in my classmates, and the heated debate it began among us. The concept was new to me, but I nonetheless took my professor's position, arguing that, of course, our experience of the world was subjective. I felt that extrapolating our experience onto others was ignorant at best, violent at worst, and missed an opportunity to consider the emptiness of our own cultural assumptions. For me this entirely new way of considering the world was exciting, but to others it felt violent, and one student in particular became incensed. He refused to accept the foreign-sounding concept of "no-self," insisting that every human being must experience the same concept of "self" as he did, and that without distinct and overt attention to the development of the self in society, there would be breakdowns in human rights. For me the conversation was an exercise in letting go; a way to consider the validity of another system of beliefs without judgment, and so I argued that when the good of the society was valued over the self, there would be an opportunity for different, not *better*, kinds of freedoms.

As the debate went on, my friend became more and more incensed. His face went red and the veins in his forehead bulged as he tried to convince us we were wrong—we *had* to be wrong—which is when it became clear to me how we are all emotionally attached *and ready to defend* who we are when it comes to our identity stories. We are raised to understand ourselves according to beliefs and practices particular to our cultural, societal, and familial experiences, which we understand more deeply by comparing and contrasting them against those who are not like us and, more often than not, determining that our way is "right" and the other way is "wrong." We can see this in common cultural dichotomies in the United States such as Christianity versus Islam, Democracy versus Communism, and Liberal versus Conservative. When we are confronted with challenges to the hegemony of our beliefs, some of us may be open to considering that we are wrong without getting defensive, but the great majority of people jump to defend their identities as if they are under attack, like my friend in Rosemont's living room back in 2000.

In writing this recollection of my professor's class, I googled Henry Rosemont (who has passed away) and found that he became a contributor to the Huffington Post in his final years. He wrote a 2-part series of articles in 2016 entitled "Capitalist Ideology and the Myth of the Individual Self," which continued to explore the same concept he introduced to us so many years before.[29] In one of these articles, he contends that the Confucian values of the Chinese people laid the foundations for them to have an entirely different experience of "the self" than the West. Confucianism, he explains, created a value system of deference and care, which is centered around the roles we occupy in relation to others, such as mother, father, sister, brother, aunt, uncle, student, teacher, and so forth. For example, in Confucian societies children are taught to defer to their elders. On one hand, this deference is taught as a proper and logical way of being because our elders are the people who care for us and it is incumbent upon us to show gratitude for this. On the other hand, this deference is culturally imbedded through the deference modeled by every child's parents toward their grandparents' parents. Deference is also expected to be given to those who care for us, including aunts, uncles, close family friends, teachers, police officers, and so on. Through deference to those who care for us, children are taught to value closeness of family, friends, and, indeed, all other humans over the self; in this conception of identity, the "self" as an autonomous, independent being is not necessary to the building of a harmonious society.

For Rosemont, this is a beautiful thing because it centralizes our interconnection to other human beings, and our relationships become what brings us meaning. He contends, and I agree, that this is a way of thinking more likely to result in the transformative change we need. This is because the major issues we face today are not individualized issues of personal freedom requiring us to value ourselves over all else; rather, we are being challenged by global issues like climate change and world peace, which require us to work together, and to value the group over the individual. When we consider the state of the world and the challenges we face, it becomes clear that a society that values personal freedoms above all else, and raises the idea of an autonomous, individual self above the needs of the group, is no longer realistic or in keeping with the realities of our lives.

While the Western understanding of self teaches us to value our individual accomplishments above all else, and to look inward for value, the Confucian understanding of self teaches that we are nothing without our relationships. In this conception, other people are not merely contingent on our self-worth, or our goal of being *good* or *human*; rather, our relationships with and behavior toward other people are integral to any idea of self-worth or humanity we are able to imagine. As Rosemont writes, "[m]y life can only have meaning as I contribute to the meaningfulness of the lives of others, and they to me. Indeed, they confer personhood on me, and do so continuously."[30] In this understanding of the self, the roles we play in the lives of others become necessary to our sense of value and accomplishment. This includes our professional and personal lives. If we are teachers, the role we play in the lives of our students will be *necessary* for our self-worth. If we are government officials, it is the role we play in the lives of our country's citizens, and so on and so forth, from our roles as parents and children to our roles as professionals and citizens. If we work in 7-11, then the happiness of our customers will be essential, and so on and so forth. In such a world, we don't work for our selfish interest (as Adam Smith envisioned), but for the interest of the larger human society. Such a conception envisions each human being as interwoven into a larger, interdependent whole, which cannot be said to be healthy or good until the majority of people's needs are considered and attended to.

Imagining such a thing in today's self-centered Western cultural imaginary is hard to do, but understanding the concept of "self" as cultural helps us to envision this concept more rationally. If our very conception of "the self" is culturally inherited, passed down through a historical evolution of ideas, which has inculcated itself into our schools, families, and ways of knowing, then *what else* about our lives has been formed in this way? And doesn't this mean that we should look upon every idea we have inherited—from who we are, to how we view the world around us—as a story we are living? If we did not choose these stories ourselves, why should we accept them so easily, without examination? Why not consider them objectively, then reframe and refocus according to the people we want to be? If stories shape our lives, let's take back the power of the narrative voice and use that power to create more meaningful, morally responsible, engaged lives that honor all living things!

What Is Valuable?

The plastics industry operates unapologetically within a value system defined by profitability, as the aforementioned story reflects. Similarly, our media and government agencies define the value of various industries and businesses according to their contribution to **our GDP** and the **number of jobs they produce**. For example, NPR's "All Things Considered" called America's agricultural industry "one of [our] success stories."[31] NPR note the total projected profits on exports ($139.5 billion in 2013, the time of the broadcast) and the fact that they support "more than 1 million jobs" as the main highlights. These numbers are impressive, and no one can argue with the way big agriculture has transformed our ability to provide affordable produce to all corners of the world; however, these numbers are not ultimately reflective of the entire truth. As anyone familiar with the environmental movement knows, the total cost of an industry is incomplete if it does not include an assessment of its impact on both our health and the environment.

According to the UN's Environmental Programme, for example, industrialized farming costs the environment a rough equivalent of $3 trillion a year in gas emissions, air/water pollution, and the destruction of wildlife.[32] A 2021 Rockefeller Foundation report breaks this down for the United States, pointing out that the country spends $1.1 trillion on food directly as a nation.[33] However, this number does not include the $2.1 trillion spent on related human health problems, such as diet-related diseases ($1.1 trillion); greenhouse gas emissions and biodiversity loss ($900 billion); and costs borne by the marginalized communities, which overwhelmingly comprise Big Agriculture's workforce through the impact of their low wages, lack of healthcare benefits, and child labor ($100 billion).

The truth is that our current national and international value system—used by most governments for assessing industry—stops at financial concerns, such as GDP and job creation. As both national and international reports make clear, however, these numbers ignore a plethora of other costs that are *not only financial*, but also *ecological* and *health-related*, not to mention emotional and psychological. And, of course, the industries concerned stretch well beyond Big Agriculture. According to the Environmental Protection Agency, industrialized agriculture accounted for approximately "10.5 percent of greenhouse gas emissions in 2018," with the rest of the emissions being made up by the general category of "industry" (28.9%); then transportation (28.3%); then commercial enterprises (16%); and finally residential concerns (15.6%).[34] In short, nearly every aspect of our modern-day lives are contributing to ecological and environmental destruction, yet we plow forward, unwilling to let go of the **convenience** we receive in return.

At the risk of fatiguing you, dear reader, with yet another of our globally unsustainable practices, I hope you will bear with me for just one more: the clothing industry. Unfortunately, the clothing industry is yet another grossly unsustainable and ecologically destructive area of concern. International and national clothing companies are quickly expanding their reach, their affordability, and therefore their waste, leading to what many are calling a culture of "fast-fashion," which is resulting in barely used cheap clothing filling landfills with tons of non-biodegradable materials each year. What many of us don't realize is that polyester, which can be seen in a large proportion of cheap clothing, is sometimes carcinogenic; or that the chemical injected into cotton to decrease wrinkles is formaldehyde.[35] In addition, cotton requires copious amounts of water and the intense use of chemical fertilizers to be grown, further adding to environmental and health costs. In 2015, greenhouse gas emissions from the global textile industry was estimated at about 1.2 billion tons of CO_2, which is "more than the emissions of all international flights and maritime shipping combined."[36]

As the Rockefeller report on Big Ag hinted at above, in addition to environmental costs there are, as always, issues of inequality. Workers are employed in sweatshops with insufficient safety protections and excessively low wages, mostly in countries like Bangladesh, India, China, Vietnam, and Ethiopia. Animals are trapped, held in cages, and slaughtered for the use of their fur and skin to make coats, shoes, and accessories. Given that producing a pound of cultivated silk "requires the death of 3,000 silkworms," which are often "dropped into boiling water to avoid the breakage of the silk when they leave the cocoon," it is clear that our global clothing industry—not to mention agriculture—does not include the life, safety, or suffering of animals as an important value.

So, let me propose the question of this chapter to you:

What is valuable?

The answer of our industries and governments seems clear: GDP and employment rates are their top concern. But such a narrowly defined value system is not working—not for the health of the planet; not for the animals, rivers, mountains, or air; and not for the people . . . especially those in marginalized communities who often bear the brunt of the negative impact.

Suggested Reflective Activity #2: Considering Our Values and Our Denial

We invite you to FREE WRITE on any or all of the following questions:

PART A: Considering Our Value System:

1. For you personally: *What is valuable?*
2. What **stories are being told** in your culture/society about what is *desirable* or *valuable* to work for, live for, or strive to attain?

   ○ Building upon your answer to the aforementioned question, reflect now on the kind of society this value system seems set up to produce, and whether or not it will get us where we need to be.

3. Considering your responses to the aforementioned questions, write in response to the following . . .

   - Are your personal values in or out of sync with those of society?
   - Remembering that what we *believe* and what we *do* can be two very different things, consider the following:

     - In what ways are you ***truly and honestly*** living according to your values?
     - In what ways is your life ***truly and honestly*** out of balance with your values?
     - In the places where you are out of balance, list one to two reasonable ways you could make positive change . . .

PART B: Considering Cognitive Dissonance:

4. To what extent are you, or those around you, engaged in cognitive dissonance?
   To answer this question, you might try the following:

   ○ List all of the daily or semi-regular activities you, or those around you, engage in that are contributing to the destruction of the planet.
   ○ Consider how—if at all—you justify these activities to yourself . . . Is there a story you are telling yourself about *why* engaging in these behaviors is acceptable? If so, what is it? Or if you do not bother to tell yourself any story at all, then try freewriting on *why* this is something you don't think about.

Scene 2

OUR CONNECTION WITH THE EARTH
AND LOVE FOR NONHUMANS

As the taxi speeds away from Beijing, toward the Great Wall, the smog from the city slowly begins to clear from the mountains and the sky becomes a lighter, brighter shade of blue. Back in the city, the app on my phone that measures parts per million of pollutants in the air was reading nearly 150, which the app tells me is "unhealthy for sensitive groups." While this is not as bad as the (relatively common) readings of 200 or 250, which can be labelled "hazardous," it is enough to make exercising outside a questionable activity (although I've never seen any of this stop native Beijingers). To put Beijing in context, the World Health Organization reports that "almost all of the global population (99%) breathe air that exceeds WHO guideline limits," and that air pollutants are associated with "7 million premature deaths annually."[1]

By the time the taxi reaches the entrance at Mutiyanu, which is one of the more commercialized entrances to the Great Wall, I can feel that the air has become more like the clean, crisp, breathable air I am used to in the United States. This excites me, and as I weave my way through the crowds at the entrance to the hike, I become eager to start the thirty-minute climb to the top. I can take full, heavy inhalations as I climb without feeling like I am being poisoned. I can sweat and push myself happily. Around me, the landscape comes to life; instead of dusty roads and thin, sickly-looking trees, there is a lush forest of green that cascades down the cliffs and around this ancient place. Because I have been reading Susan Griffin's "Split Culture" (1989) on the taxi ride up to the mountains, I already have a question in mind: Are we *a part of* nature? Is it in us, and us in it? Is this essential connection part of what is being overlooked in today's culture?

I wonder, as I run my hands over the reconstructed stones that line the stairs and look out over the mountains that stretch out around me, if the men who struggled to carry these stones felt connected to the earth or the people around them as they worked. Many of them died during the process, a testament to the relentless determination of humans to protect their borders and ward off invaders from neighboring countries.

In some ways, the Great Wall is a symbol of the lengths we are forced to go to protect ourselves from the desire of other humans—the desire for expansion, domination, and power that has driven so much of human history. Although we invade and conquer less in our modern world, we can still see these seeds of human greed in the relentless expansion of industry, which is spurred not by what humans *need*, but by what they will pay money for. In the process, we continue to develop a global culture of competition based around money and power. This begs the question: Why has our species taken so long to evolve from a place of competition and *power over* others? Even as we developed systems that made competition for food and shelter unnecessary, what is it that has continued to drive us to see humans with different skin colors, religious beliefs, and languages as *others*? Why have our governments remained so steeped in a culture of fear, pushed to continually create weapons of war, erect boundaries, point out differences, and establish dominance before the "other" can do it first? What is it that leads us to fight, rather than smile at, a stranger?

> **Jing**: The Great Wall was the human endeavor to stop "invaders" from taking our land and properties including human beings (as laborers). We have built up walls that separated each other all around the world, and walls that separate us from nature. We are walled in buildings so that nature is kept outside; we are walled in cities so that we do not see the majestic sunrise and sunset in the skyline anymore. How many walls are there in the world? How many are we still building? How many walls have we erected in our hearts to guard against others?! Can we reconceptualize our world and build bridges instead? Bridges of love, and bridges of understanding . . .

It is important to recognize that alongside our global stories of war and division, a deep capacity for empathy, love, and compassion is also present in human beings. We see this in the way we are there for one another during emergencies, and in our personal and family stories. But too often our capacity for love and care is limited to people who look like us, stopping at artificial borders and boundaries. A less common example of this disregard is the dismissive attitude we have toward nonhumans. Animals—especially "farm animals"—as well as rivers, forests, mountains, and oceans. We may appreciate the natural, nonhuman world as beautiful, or comforting in times of trouble, but few of us look at it as a living being deserving of health, happiness, and the right to life, the same as human beings.

Imagining Ourselves Into the Lives of Others: Less Obvious Habits of Violence

Not so long ago I was home with my parents for a short break. As we were driving down the highway in Maryland on a hot summer's day, we got stuck behind a chicken truck. From four or five car-lengths away you could see tufts of white feathers trailing behind it into the street. The smell was almost unbearable—like rotten eggs mixed with feces. When we finally passed, we saw the chickens, three or four to a plastic crate, unable to stand, beaks pressed against the grates. Even my parents, who have never considered giving up meat, had trouble looking at the truck openly.

I now occasionally eat meat, but over the six years that I was vegetarian (1999–2005), I often fielded a barrage of defensive comments from dining partners who took my vegetarianism personally. The most common remark, often delivered with a sarcastic smile, was that *eating meat is natural*, because *we are part of the food chain*. To this I would agree, then counter with the observation that *we now have the knowledge and ability to rise above the food chain, so why don't we?* This usually ended the conversation.

I became a vegetarian after attending a talk about pacifism at my undergraduate university where images of young children helping their parents slaughter animals were flashed on the screen as evidence of a culture of violence bubbling beneath the surface. One image in particular hit me in my gut; twenty years later I can still see it clearly: *a boy of no more than eight or nine stands on a dock by the sea with his back to the camera. He is beside his father and a group of other men busily hauling in a whale. One of the boy's arms hangs loose at his side, and in it is a bloodied knife he has presumably just used to slice at the whale, whose carcass floats lifelessly on the water. The men gather around their kill, pleased with their prize, which will be cut up and sold for a high price. All the while the knife is dripping with thick red blood, and the young boy holds it so casually.*

Looking at that picture, the connection the speakers made between eating meat and violence in our society seemed right to me—I believed in pacifism and peace, so why was I taking part in violence against animals, which appeared every night on my dinner plate? This led me to the belief that I should not eat anything I couldn't stand to kill, or which I couldn't at least *watch* being killed, because otherwise I was taking part in a system that I knew, in my gut, wasn't right.

For the next six years I didn't think about eating, or even come close to craving, meat. My vegetarianism came to an unexpected end when it was determined that I needed surgery to fix a shattered knee, but I was so anemic they had to delay the surgery. They put me on a regimen of iron pills and my doctor begged me to start eating red meat. If I were given the same news today, I would counter the suggestion that meat is the only way to raise iron levels, but I was a young twenty-six-year-old in the midst of a traumatic experience. When my parents, concerned about my health, joined the chorus, I felt pushed to try. I was crestfallen that my body seemed to *need* meat, but I did start to eat it again. As I reentered the meat-eating world, however, I was determined to at least eat meat ethically. I preferred that the animals I ate were raised on small farms where they had some quality of life, and where I at least wasn't complicit in the industrialized food system, and I retained the feeling that I should not be eating something that I could not stand to watch being killed. That is why, years later, when some friends asked if I wanted to pitch in to buy a whole pig, I asked if it would be possible to watch the pig be butchered, thinking this would be the perfect opportunity to see if I could stand watching an animal being killed for me to eat when that animal had been raised on a farm rather than in a factory.

We drove up to the farm early one morning and walked around to the back of the farm where the pigs had been rounded up for slaughter that day. There were about six full-sized pigs in the open air with miles of green grass all around them, but they had been rounded up for slaughter today, and so they were in a small square of dirt penned off with a wooden fence. Each had a thick collar around its neck, cool pink skin, big floppy ears that fell into its eyes, and the trademark curly cue tail you see in cartoon depictions. Beside the pen was a box truck, its rolling metal door gaping open, outfitted with three large metal hooks on the reinforced cross beam. Around the truck were three men dressed in slick, rubbery pants and long rubber aprons. One by one the pigs were dragged away from the other pigs by their collars and shot quickly in the forehead with a bolt gun. They died immediately. They were then hung upside down on one of the metal hooks from the back of the truck and in the expert hand of the butcher, they were skinned, gutted, and drained of blood in a matter of minutes. They were then cut up in the open air, in front of all the other pigs with whom they had been penned in mere moments earlier.

The pigs who remained, watching their companions being dragged out one by one, were squealing frantically. They were not acting chaotically—running around, trying to escape—but stayed pushed together, as if there were safety in numbers, huddled against the same part of the pen where my friends and I were standing. Their faces stayed like that, smashed against the fence, looking up at us, begging for us to help them. I mean, that's what it seemed like to me. Their eyes were on mine. They were looking right at me. To this day I can still see the face of the pig at the center of the group, its eyes gripping mine, overcome with terror. It seemed as if they could feel what I was feeling, which was compassion, regret, and something akin to an out-of-body experience, and so I leaned down and put my hand on a few of their heads and I swear that calmed them.

I had no doubt that they knew what was coming. When I asked how old the pigs were, hoping that at least they had lived to a ripe old age, I was told six months . . . that was the age when they were full-grown, and could now fetch the highest price. In the eyes of the farmer, the pig was still a commodity, not a sentient being just as worthy of living its life as any human would be. To make matters even more complicated, my roommate—who was a sound technician—had come along to record the sound of squealing pigs. He felt that it was a rare opportunity to capture a sound he could make use of in his projects; looking back on this, I realize now that the "squealing" he was capturing was their fear and anxiety . . . it was almost as if their slaughter, and the fear and anxiety they felt as they faced it, was there for our entertainment. Not knowing what else to do, my friends and I looked at one another and laughed, feeling the tension, knowing we were complicit in the slaughter, and doing it anyway.

It was one of the more complicated moments of my life, because I was trying to do something good for my iron levels, for animals, and for the environment. I was buying a whole animal from a small farm owner who, compared to industrial farmers, took care of his animals. I was removing myself from the industrialized food system in the process. But being there that day and witnessing the pigs crammed together in the pen as they were slaughtered in front of their companions, one after another, made it absolutely clear that no matter how small the farm, the core business of eating meat was the killing of sentient beings, who have all the same rights to life as I do. And yet without meat, I find it terribly difficult to eat a well-balanced, healthy diet with plenty of iron and vitamin B.

Left to my own devices, I eat animal meat only when I feel my body craving it, which is about once every two to three weeks; but I still eat it. Sometimes when I am out with friends, there will be hardly any other option. If I chose to think about the animal who sacrificed its life every time I brought a forkful of meat to my mouth, I would not be able to get it down, which makes me wonder what kind of spiritual imbalance I perpetuate each time I accomplish this feat of psychological gymnastics . . . and what kind of havoc it is wreaking on my body.

> **Jing**: Amanda's experience is heart-wrenching. I face the same kind of dilemma. After I started on meditation, I gave up my fishing hobby as I distinctly felt the pain of the hook in the mouth of the fish. I gave up on meat and I was vegan for fourteen years until being diagnosed as very anemic. I decided to eat some meat for my health. Once after I come back from a buffet, in my heart I heard the most horrifying cries of animals in excruciating pain and total desperation. I also once dreamed of animals being ripped out of their skins and being boiled alive while I was vividly feeling what they felt, as if I lived in their bodies. So, I now consume some meat with a troubled conscience. I refrain from eating all red meat, but still I feel troubled and decided to consciously plan every day what to eat so that meat is consumed at the minimum level just to get enough iron.
>
> I also remember what my dear late friend Heidi Ross told me about her decision to become vegetarian after seeing the animals slaughtered in her family's farm at age fifteen. She could not bear to eat the meat of the animals she had grown up with and so loved! She remembered that the night she decided to forgo meat, thousands and thousands of animals flying from many directions came to her in her dream and stood in front of her looking at her lovingly, and they were in many beautiful colors and forms. To Heidi's surprise, I became vegan. I thought her experience of the animal dream would be just for her, until one day after a meal in which I was teased by colleagues that I wasted all the money I made (because I was forgoing the joy of eating meat), and my response was, "you become what you eat." That night, I had a vivid dream in which thousands of animals came and knelt in front of me, their eyes looking grateful. The emotions held within all of these events were extraordinarily powerful. How can we transform our food industry so that becoming and being vegan is easy?

Animals are not always put into the category of food . . . sometimes, if they are cute and fluffy enough, we upgrade them to the category of pets. We treat pets as beloved parts of our families. Not only are they a joy to be around, but they also make our homes more welcoming, our lives more full, and our burdens easier to bear. Many of my friends have pets that are quite literally part of the family—when they are sick they are taken to the doctor, and when they die they are deeply mourned.

You have probably heard about dogs being used to lift prisoners out of depression. There is a program in Florida where hard-to-adopt dogs are paired with inmates whose good behavior has earned them a chance to participate in a dog-training program. The article describes the moment that the dogs are introduced, explaining that generally "the prisoners are 'scowling and don't want to be there,' but all that changes when the moment comes that they get to interact with the pups."[2] As the article explains, this is because "the human-animal bond is very powerful," and when dogs that come from broken homes, much like the inmates themselves, are put in a vulnerable position where they need the inmates to show them love and affection, it is like a switch is flipped and the inmates show "enhanced empathy, emotional intelligence, communication, patience, self-control and trust." This underscores something that pet owners and animal lovers have always known—that when we allow animals into our hearts and lives, we will often find a surprisingly deep and meaningful emotional connection.

> **Jing**: The deep bond we have with other species could be biological. Current research finds that we share 99.7 percent genes with chimpanzees, 80 percent with cows, and even 60 percent with bugs.[3] In fact, animals are smarter than humans in many ways. Their eyes and their features all show that they are sacredly designed and equally blessed by our Creator. The deep bond with other species that we have requires us to delve deeply into the energy that creates all existence and to connect with the spirit embedded in all existence. Beyond the superficial differences, we know we belong to each other, we have been with each other, and we have been each other, as Eastern religions say we have shared many life journeys together. We are in the journey on earth together again to elevate each other and each contributes uniquely to the universe's evolution.

The slaughter of animals for meat consumption is not the only way we objectify them or disregard their well-being. Globally, we destroy their habitats, drive them from forests, jungles, and other lands so that we can extract resources and expand housing. My parents live in a sparsely woody suburban area where we sometimes see deer burst out from the thinnest patch of woods into the street because they have no more land to walk through freely. Many of us bow our heads and lament this loss of habitat for animals, but remain convinced that our houses, roads, bridges, and infrastructure always come first.

In some parts of the world animals are starting to fight back in frightening ways. A recent article in National Geographic (2020) writes about how in parts of Uganda, where lands have been cleared for crops and only patches of forest left, there have been more than forty confirmed attacks by chimpanzees on small children.[4] The chimps don't eat the children—they grab them, drag them into the forest, kill them, and leave them to die—like a warning. In some cases, they terrorize families, coming again and again to their houses, waiting for an opportune moment. But more often these attacks happen by chimps who act recklessly in a moment of seeming insanity that becomes fatal; it is rare for such an action to be repeated by the same chimp. What is happening seems clear to me: they have little left and they are desperate, so they are acting out in a frenzied panic, possibly hoping that they can scare us enough to leave them alone. This is something many of us—if our homes were being destroyed and our family's lives were at stake—can probably imagine doing. Not in a premeditated way, but in our darkest moments of desperation, if our lives and the lives of those we loved were being threatened. Why, when it is chimps whose homes and families are threatened, are we so much less understanding?

There is no easy solution to human expansion, especially in the Global South. People clear forests and plant crops because they need more money to live and feed their families, just like oil rig and coal mine workers go to work every day because they need a paycheck. When we reimagine our world, we will have to accept that ethical change is not going to be easy. It will require sacrifice and attention to the inequalities inherent in the development of the Global South, when the Global North has already wreaked its fair share of destruction. But regardless of what we do, our guiding principles should be rooted in virtue, value, and the compassionate, humane treatment of *all* living beings. Not wealth. Not power or control. Not a human-centered view of existence that disregards and devalues all other things. Not historical vendettas or competition between human beings. Let's put these values at the center, then work outward carefully.

Jing: If we can put ourselves into the shoes of animals, we will not dare to do what we do. What if it is humans who were put in cages and locked up in zoos to be observed by other nonhuman species? What if we were given electric shocks or forced to play with fire for the cheers of nonhuman species, or our parts were cut off to serve as medicines, or burned and roasted for "delicious" food? The inability to "inter-be" keeps us numb. The pain needs to be felt in the flesh to wake us up. Contemplative practices such as meditation can sensitize our body to feel for each other and other species, and when we fully open up our life force to connect with other life forces, we cannot bear to imagine doing what we are doing now to other species! Also, we have enough resources if we share equally for what humans need rather than for what they want. Instead of expansion, we can redistribute resources and have peace and justice on Earth guided by the principles of compassion and respect for each other. The system we have now on Earth has to be transformed.

As we discussed in Scene 1, our stories around "progress" and "success" and "wealth" lead us to value unfettered expansion and wealth accumulation above other things, allowing destructive industries such as oil drilling and industrialized agriculture to continue without responsible regulations. We continue to shamelessly profit from the sale of weapons of war, engage in hiking the prices of pharmaceuticals, and drag our feet on improved public transportation systems to keep industry leaders happy. We label those industrial activities that pollute our water, soil, and air as economic investments integral to economic growth rather than what they are—symptoms of our scrambled sense of right and wrong.

The people running these destructive industries are not bad people. Those who tirelessly fight to keep fossil fuels flowing at all costs—even as their actions rush us closer to climate catastrophe—are not evil or incapable of empathy or love. But they have been, it seems, blinded by the need to accumulate, having fully bought into our cultural stories about success. This is not a surprising response to a global society whose laws, media, and societal structures value the accumulation of wealth over nearly everything, including human rights, biodiversity, and the health of the planet. When I ask myself what has the power to help people see beyond their own selfish interests in order to put the Earth first and save us from climate chaos, *the only thing that seems feasible to consider is a spiritual awakening.* Logic alone isn't going to do it—

we know this because we already have all the science we need, and the information has been widely disseminated. What remains out of reach is the emotional and spiritual strength to recognize right and wrong despite the financial rewards created by our upside-down system.

Suggested Reflective Activity #3: Considering Nonhumans

We invite you to FREE WRITE on any or all of the following questions:

- Imagine the world you hope will be here for future generations—describe what people will be able to see, feel, hear, and experience as they go on walks through the land, along the sea, or through their own neighborhoods.

  - To what extent does the natural world come to mind in this scenario?
  - What is the role of nonhumans?

- What is your opinion about the rights of animals in the face of human expansion and development?

  - Should the rights of animals be considered?
  - What about the rights of trees, mountains, streams, and oceans?

- Do you feel differently about dogs and cats than you do about other kinds of animals, like pigs and cows? If so, why?

  - Is there anything "wrong" with people in South Korea and China eating dog meat?
  - Why do we snub our noses (Americans, at least) at eating horse meat?

- If we organized our lives around a truly egalitarian ethic, which values the life of all sentient things, including humans and nonhumans, what would we feel moved to change?

Scene 3

THE WESTERN CULTURAL IMAGINARY
STORIES THAT TAUGHT US TO VALUE
THE MIND OVER THE BODY

A family member of mine has contended, on multiple occasions, that Europeans must have been "more advanced" than the native peoples they enslaved or drove nearly to extinction because otherwise they would not have been able to conquer them so easily. This person, whom I love dearly, contends that our ability to build ships capable of navigating the seas, and cannons and guns capable of killing from a distance, combined with our desire to conquer distant people and lands, is evidence of advanced thinking.

This characterization of military might as evidence of intelligence is, I believe, shared by many. But is it really a mark of superiority to have developed weapons of war? Can we really call that which led us to conquer distant lands, callously, selfishly, and despicably throwing asunder foreign civilization, *intelligence?* Perhaps, instead, it was a misplaced value system (power and domination over integration and love) that drove us to create this kind of machinery. And perhaps it was a deficiency of emotional awareness and empathy that allowed us to carry it out on comparatively defenseless people.

If we were to judge the conquerors' intelligence on a moral or emotional scale, there is no question where they would rank. What was done during the colonial period not only killed and enslaved swaths of innocent people, but also laid the groundwork for wars over land and religion, which continue to ravage entire countries and regions to this day. It created a system of global power dynamics, with those countries who benefitted the most from colonialism continuing to occupy an outsized role in international institutions, as well as a comparatively stable economic and political situation compared to those who were colonized.[1] If we valued emotional, moral, ecological, and spiritual intelligence the way we value the intelligence that allows us to create powerful weapons of war, how might our view of history change?

Historically, the Western conception of Nature is a complicated one. The etymology of the word "wilderness" is explained by Professor David Henderson as a combination of the Old English word for *beast* (deor) and the word for *wild* (wilde) to form *wilddeor,* or "wild animal."[2] From *wilddeor* eventually came *wilderness.* For Henderson, the centrality of wild animals in the evolution of the word *wilderness* "points not only to the absence of human culture in the landscape but to the presence of that which is often incompatible with it," establishing a view of nature as in opposition to, perhaps even in direct conflict with, humans.

Native American author, historian, lawyer, and activist Vine Deloria Jr. recalls the European's association of *wilderness* with that which is *inhospitable* in his essay, *American Indians and Wilderness.* He writes that the categorization of the natural world as something "wild," which needed to be tamed—rather than something mysterious and beautiful which should be respected and learned from—is particular to Europeans.[3] While the first European colonists described the New World as "howling," "dismal," and "terrible," Native Americans saw the same natural landscape they lived in as bountiful, overflowing with the blessings of "the Great Mystery," and the "the seamless web of life." This view of the natural world as something to be respected and learned from is how, Deloria contends, Native Americans thought of the natural world that surrounded them, showing a distinct difference in the intellectual and emotional regard of Native Americans for nature when compared to European colonizers.

Deloria offers a particularly resonant example of ways that Native Americans looked toward nature as a teacher and guide when moving from one piece of land to another in the quote below. He writes about their tricks for learning about a foreign landscape, explaining that

> newcomers would be particularly interested in trying to orient themselves to the behavior of the living beings already present on the land, trying to model their actions after the animals they saw around them and by so doing adapt themselves to the new landscape. In this respect, we see the Indian belief that humans are not the highest product of the creation or even of evolution. Instead, they fall short in many ways. They're not as fast as the four leggeds, not able to fly like the birds, not as keen of eye as the hawks and eagles, not as strong as the buffalo or bears . . . consequently, we needed to develop alliances with other beings that had been here longer and that possessed better physical attributes and had more wisdom than we.

In Deloria's description, Native Americans were able, due to their way of seeing and thinking, to harness the bear's energy and wisdom while respecting its power, benefitting from a symbiotic relationship founded on a view of humans and animals as equally valuable. What a formidable instinct it was to look at a bear and want to understand and learn from it rather than hide from it or kill it!

The Native American conception of the Earth as a teacher seems logical since without the Earth—without its atmosphere, its bounty of plants and animals, its source of fresh water and fertile soil—we could not survive. It also seems spiritual in the sense that their idea of *teacher* allowed for a kind of learning that requires humans to let go of their own ego and consider the *other* as having valuable knowledge and wisdom to share. Their equating of that which gives us life to a sacred thing that holds the secret to many mysteries opened up the possibility of a belief system founded on the interconnection of the mind and body (logic and spirit), as well as humans and their surroundings. Deloria's passage is perhaps best encapsulated by a quote he includes from the late Native American civil rights leader, Standing Bear, who said that for Native Americans, "the world was a library and its books were the stones, leaves, grass, brooks, and the birds and animals that shared, alike with us, the storms and blessings of earth." In this view of nature, human's dominion over the natural world is flipped, and we become its students.

Philosophical Influence on the Western Cultural Imaginary: A Story of Duality

Among scholars who consider our separation from nature as a cultural heritage, attention is often given to the mind-body split, which is said to have occurred in the early seventeenth century with thinkers like Decartes. Hesoon Bai, in her chapter *Reanimating the Universe: Environmental Education and Philosophical Animism*, calls Descartes a symptom of a much older idea formed by Plato (428–37 BC) some three to four hundred years before Christ. Bai brings up Plato's impassioned critique of the ancient poet, Homer (long dead by the time of Plato), whose narrative poems were thought to "appeal to the sensuous experience of the listener" and to "[induce] in the latter a trance-like hypnotic state in which the listener experiences an emotional identification or merging with what was presented to them through the poet's skillful performance."[4]

Anyone of us who loves art can relate to this description—I, for one, have often been moved to a trance-like state during musical performances, readings given by especially gifted orators, or in a throng of people when I key into something captivating about a work of art. Even in a throng of people, a powerful work of art will simply transport me to what feels like a different realm of being where I am suddenly alive and vibrating with a completely different energy, maybe even a kind of wisdom. This has also happened to me during lectures, and in China as I poured over the reading for my Eco-Ethics course, which led to the writing of these pages.

During extended periods of regular meditation practice, as well as over the course of writing of this book, I have become familiar with the feeling of *spirit* in my heart and body; in so doing, I feel comfortable calling my experiences with art *spiritual experiences.* I think what makes them *spiritual* rather than *cerebral* is the rooting of those experiences in the body, and the feeling that the experience lies somewhere beyond reach; for me, the knowledge gleaned from those experiences usually comes from a place that cannot be immediately expressed in words, even for someone who fancies herself a writer. Putting my experience into words requires reflection, meditation, and time wrestling with language, after which I am able to *translate* the experience into words, often through the medium of creative description, which imitates art as closely as possible, its goal being to transport the reader into an emotional experience.

Plato, as Bai explains his thinking, rejected the spiritual experience of art on the grounds that it interrupted the individual's ability to develop their rational, analytic mind. She quotes Plato's assessment of poetry from *The Republic* (1965), where he writes that "all poetry, from Homer onwards, consists in representing a semblance of its subject . . . with no grasp of reality." She assesses his perspective on knowledge gleaned from the senses—including feelings, intuitions, and what I would call the *spiritual experience of art*—as unreal, while that which "we can know through the intellect—the faculty of conceptualization—is real." In this reading of Plato, we see him as attempting to lead a "revolution of human consciousness" which devalued sense-based knowing and privileged that which could be proven—discursive, intellectually derived knowing.

In Plato's famous Theory of Forms, he posits what some understand to be a distinction between True, Real knowledge (purposefully capitalized) and knowledge which is corrupted by that which cannot be trusted—i.e., the senses. Plato's famous analogy of the Cave reinforces this concept—

people chained in a cave facing the wall may think that the shadows passing across the cave's wall are the "real world," but in Truth they are only being fooled by the unreliable, limited knowledge of their senses. In talking about the connection between the "real world of Forms" and poetry, he writes that "if wisdom is to be gained only through knowledge of the real world of Forms" (as Plato argued it should be), then "the claim that the poet can educate mankind to virtue must be as hollow as the pretense that the artist knows all about shoemaking because he can paint a lifelike picture of a shoemaker."⁵ What is important about this brief summary of Plato's ideas is the question they planted about the reliability of the senses, leading to the emergence of a hierarchy of one form of Truth or Reality over another: logic over the senses.

Bai attributes this hierarchy of ideas, planted by Plato in the Western cultural imaginary, to the development of Descartes' theory of substance. Descartes' theory of substance held that the universe was made of two distinct substances: mental substances (the faculties of the mind), and matter (meaning the physical existence of the body). This implies that the body and mind are distinct. Because thinkers at the time valued *the mind* as the highest form of human existence, this meant that for Descartes (and the body of Western thought that built upon his ideas), the body was degraded as less than the mind, and eventually as no better than empty physical space, without essential value. This led to a false dualism that idealized the mind and not only degraded the physical world, but also repositioned the senses—our experiences of taste, touch, sound, and smell, the experience of love, joy, beauty, and so forth—in the *mind*, which Descartes saw as the only part of us undefined and untouched by the emptiness of matter.

One application of Descartes' hierarchy of the mind over matter was the idea that true knowledge—which represents all that is good and valuable—comes from the mind alone. As such, knowledge gleaned from the body, or Nature, was not to be trusted. In this understanding of the world, Nature cannot be an animated part of existence with its own life-force or energy. It cannot be a powerful source of wisdom or a repository of essential knowledge, as the Native Americans see it, and it certainly cannot be responsible for any sort of transformative experience, because any experience that is good or true would be rooted in the mind.

For me, this is a familiar idea . . . even a familiar niggling at the back of my mind when I listen to people talking about the power of the trees, or the knowledge they gleaned from looking at the stars. This stripping of inherent knowledge from the "object world" is a Western idea deeply embedded in our cultural heritage. It is a cultural understanding of Nature as matter alone—without spirit—which makes it easy to dismiss those who insist that trees have a personality, or that the ocean is vibrating with love, as illogical or out of touch with reality. Those who have taken this view of Nature as their own will reject out of hand the long-held beliefs of Native Americans and Eastern thinkers who see humans and the natural world as interconnected and mutually dependent, preferring to retain what has become a comforting feeling of superiority over all nonhuman beings.

It seems clear to me (Amanda) that we *still* operate in a world where the logical outshines, and is valued *over*, the spiritual and the sensual. We continue to devalue knowledge from nature, art, and meditation while raising up the knowledge gleaned from "objective data" and science as comparatively trustworthy and reliable. Yet, this same data is not enough to convince us to change the way we live, making its shortcomings painfully obvious. For Bai, the influence of the mind-body split created by Plato and Descartes (whom she calls the "Grand Architects of Western Thought") has been "decisive, immense, and enduring," ultimately leading to the stripping of animation, or consciousness, from the natural world, and saddling us with a deeply felt, culturally ingrained suspicion of knowledge gleaned from sensory experience. This includes personal spiritual experiences of art, as well as wisdom gleaned from ancient traditions, like that of the Native Americans, who see the nonhuman world as teachers. These culturally inherited suspicions teach us to cut ourselves off from certain ways of feeling, seeing, and knowing. In so doing we risk overlooking a universe of essential knowledge that is always at our fingertips.

What's important about this discussion is not whether this interpretation of Plato or Descartes is correct, but the articulation of a Western cultural imaginary deeply rooted in the concept of a mind-body split. It is not difficult to see the continuation of this bias toward "objective knowledge" over corporeal or spiritual knowledge in the world today. I see it in academia, which values quantitative over qualitative research; and in environmental politics, where we rely almost entirely on the science and data-driven arguments to make our point. This way of thinking and being leaves us at an enormous disadvantage, operating with only part of the faculties we have been gifted in this world to understand, connect, and make decisions.

Jing: In my view, both Plato and Descartes have also emphasized
the spiritual part of our being and knowledge, but with science

being dominant and scientists holding onto science as the absolute way of knowing, these aspects in their thoughts were neglected and forgotten. In my understanding, the realm of Ideas in Plato's work could also be the realm of Spirits, and Descartes indicated that there is a divine consciousness behind the mind and within ourselves. Similarly, Newton is often lumped into the camp of scientists who posit a mechanical universe, but Newton was an alchemist whose insights must have resulted from looking deeply into the secret of our body, mind, heart, and spirit, the secret of the universe.

What Are We Missing Out On?

Imagine you are a person who has been trained—by your culture, by the expectations of your teachers, your job, and the values of your society— to value the logical, thinking mind over the emotional one. This training, over time, becomes a belief system, consistently reinforced by the established habits and patterns created by repetition—the firing of neural pathways in the same way over and over—underscored by the incessant messages we are exposed to about what is *good*, and *rational*, and *right*. In this way, the foundational belief systems of the culture we are raised in have a profound power over the kinds of thinking, being, and believing we invest ourselves in, versus the kinds of thinking, being, and believing we dismiss outright.

By and large, we live in a world that dismisses the idea of *communicating* with nature (really communicating). We live in a society in which saying you have learned something important from the feeling of the breeze on your skin, or the experience of an amazing art exhibit, is too often dismissed with a sarcastic laugh or a knowing grin. But some of the most beautiful and important work we do comes from the sensual world of our emotions. For example, as a writer my creative capacity depends on my ability to turn off my logical, thinking mind and enter a quiet state where words flow onto the page without examination. Despite the ways I've trained myself to enter this state on command, melting into the natural world, and settling into a place beyond thought, require a conscious decision that my thinking brain fights. Sometimes, when I walk through nature, I find it difficult to turn off my thinking brain, breathe deeply, and actually *sink into* the beauty around me. I can't help but wonder if the difficulty I experience in turning off my thinking brain is in part due to the fact that I belong to a culture that does not value—let alone teach—ways to raise up the inner energy of my corporeal being and sit comfortably in its energy.

The danger in dismissing corporeal and spiritual knowledge as *unreliable* and *less than* is that we risk not only degrading people's interest in residing in their nonthinking mind, but also, more troublingly, to reject its most intriguing mysteries. The majority of our schools do not mention knowledge besides that found in books, and rarely offer courses that take students out into the natural world to learn from nonhumans as teachers. Our politicians do not talk about the importance of valuing the air, land, and water as equal beings, but, instead, root solutions to the environmental crisis in terms of technological advances and the economy. This is because the major cultural streams that we tap into are not enriched by the deep mysteries of the body, heart, and spirit, but reside almost entirely in the mind. We have not spent time developing tools for switching from a state of mind-centered knowing to a heart- or spirit-centered one, and we certainly do not condone teaching such things to children in schools. So, what are we missing out on by not giving equal weight to this wealth of spiritual, embodied knowledge? What if we were raised in an entirely different cultural imaginary? One that valued spiritual understanding and logical thinking equally? How different would our lives be?

> **Jing**: We have two brains: the right brain and the left brain. The left brain is valued by science and our society largely. It is the logical, linear, thinking brain, while our right brain is the feeling, creative brain connected to other beings and people. Our right brain is largely neglected and suppressed. Just look at how little time arts education is granted around the world. Our brain also has a pineal gland that can open us to the many dimensions of the world, but it is largely dormant as we are so pinned on the narrow lens of the mind. Meditation brings energy to the front lobe and can activate this organ called the Third Eye, the wisdom eye to cosmic wisdom. Scientific research is catching up now to find that we are using only less than 10 percent of our brain, and also that our brain is effectively connected with our heart. Our heart is found to have ten times higher electromagnetic energy than the brain, and, in fact, the heart can think. Imagine if we have a paradigm shift and explore our body and our heart and mind holistically, what kind of new humans we will have!

An Ending: Bringing It Back to the Stories We Tell

As we have shown so far in Act I, the world has been understood, shaped, and driven by well-told stories. From early Western philosophers such as Plato and Descartes, to Judeo-Christian theologists, to thinkers like Adam Smith and Confucius, who put forward ideas about the highest human good that continue to influence us to this day, our cultural imaginary is made from powerful ideas formed into captivating narratives. These narratives shape belief systems, bond nations, spark revolutions, and lead armies.

Powerful stories can be leveraged to create monumental impacts and enormous change. The Communist Revolution in China told a story about the subjugation of the proletariat by the bourgeoisie. Hitler told a story about Jews being the source of all of Germany's problems. The original colonizers of Europe told stories about the "white man's burden" to educate and civilize a world of dark-skinned savages overseas. Slave traders told stories about the inhuman Black race in need of order and discipline. Abolitionists told stories about the inherent worth of every human being. Gandhi and Martin Luther King told stories about the power of nonviolence coupled with hope and dogged determinism. The current Black Lives Matter movement in the United States tells the story of systematic and long-term racial discrimination exemplified through the killing and imprisonment of Black and Brown bodies.

History is a tug of war between powerful stories. Which one rises to the top of the cultural imaginary depends on a complex web of power, privilege, compassion, and consciousness. A successful story will seize on the exigence of the moment; tap into fear, hope, or desire; and present a meaningful cause for people to commit themselves to fully. When a story is well taught and effectively spread, it will take root in our hearts as well as our minds, causing people to rise up as flag-bearers of those ideas. Through the conviction and willingness of everyday people to act, a tiny sliver of possibility is opened up and change becomes possible. But as history has shown, it is **essential** that we choose the **right story**. The wrong story has the power to catapult us into an abyss, and once we are there, it takes many lifetimes to see our way out again.

Today, the dominant global belief about the climate seems to be that we should do what we can, but without sacrificing our economic growth or life of convenience. Could we, with the proper motivation, simply choose to believe in something different? Could we find a way to replace our selfishness and greed with a new set of beliefs, reinforced by a different way of valuing experience and knowledge—a different way, even of thinking—that could help us to find the strength we need to make great sacrifices? Maybe even to end global suffering, inequality, and planetary destruction! Could we cultivate a new narrative designed to move toward equality, sustainability, and peace?

David Korten (2015), in his book *Change the Story, Change the Future: A Living Economy for a Living Earth*, makes the argument that "we cannot act coherently as a society without a shared framing story," which is why "no matter how discredited an established story may be, we cling to it in our public discourse until it is replaced by a more compelling story."[6] Korten labels our current shared story as *The Sacred Money and Markets story*, and argues that this story creates a shared belief that money is the one and only avenue for happiness, wealth, and stability. Believers in this story feel that disrupting the current market-oriented global system would be detrimental to the fabric of society, which is what makes it so hard for people to imagine any kind of change toward a sustainable energy future—because doing so requires us to first dismantle the current "framing story" and replace it with another one entirely. Yet clearly, given the rate at which we are hurtling toward devastation and chaos, *The Sacred Money and Markets* story is flawed . . . so why do people cling to it so thoughtlessly and desperately?

Korten surmises that because we need a framing story, we will not be able to let go of *The Sacred Money and Markets* story until a similarly compelling story is presented to take its place. Korten therefore proposes a *counter story*, which he calls: *A Living Economy for a Living Earth*. His proposed story is one that teaches listeners a different kind of truth: that rather than needing money or material possessions to be happy, what we actually need to be happy is a deep awareness of, and attention to, our interconnection with the Earth and all living beings, envisioned as one interconnected Earth community.

In Act II we will discuss some of our own ideas for how to envision this new relationship with Nature, reframing Her as a friendly and intimate friend capable of imbuing us, through Her gentle and boundless love, with solace, gratitude, healing, and peace. Regardless of the story we choose, one thing has been made absolutely clear by science: change *is* necessary. The problem we need to solve isn't whether or not we change the story we tell but *how* to *make the leap*, so that we can transform from complacent consumers into impassioned agents of change . . . if not publicly, then quietly, in the everyday choices we make.

Jing: There is a rapidly increasing amount of research on our consciousness, and how different levels of consciousness decide how we see things, and treat life, and manifest attributes. Beliefs are energy-guiding templates. They direct where we put our aspirations and efforts. A new belief requires inner changes as well as outer forces. The moment of change or the window of change is when the heart is telling the person this is the right thing to do and to believe. We need to have those moments of awakening and wisdom of change to transform our consciousness. We may be moving into a less materialistic culture with many new realizations about what this materialistic culture has caused the Earth to suffer. What will jolt us into a fully new consciousness is when we embody nature as a living being, and we have awe and respect for all living things. Again, I believe meditation or inner work lies at the foundation of our transformation.[7,8,9]

Suggested Reflective Activity #4: Reflecting on Inherited Stories

We invite you to FREE WRITE on any or all of the following questions:

1. What personal stories do you live and tell about the value of rational/logical thinking?

   ○ What role does rational/logical thinking play in the formation of your life and/or your relationships?

2. What stories do you live and tell about the value of the body/emotion/intuition?

   ○ What role do emotion and intuition play in the formation of your life and/or your relationships?

3. How do you *story* the natural world in your life? In other words . . .

   ○ What beliefs do you carry about the non-animal world—the forests, oceans, mountains, and soil?

     ▪ Do you believe the forests, mountains, oceans, and/or soil have consciousness? If so, in what way?
     ▪ Do you believe there is a way to communicate with the natural world? If so, how? If not, why not?

4. What stories do you live and tell about your power to create change—both in your personal life, and in the face of climate chaos?

   - Do you believe what you do matters?
   - If not you, who has the power to create change?

Act II

ENVISIONING AND PREPARING FOR THE
JOURNEY AHEAD

Scene 4

INSPIRATION

STORIES OF VISION AND CHANGE

Not too long ago I had an hour's lesson with a nine-year-old Chinese student who lives in Beijing. I had been teaching her for over a year then and we had just finished reading a book together. For the sake of variety, we decided to do a creative project before starting the next book in the series. I suggested that we design our "ideal society." I presented the activity as an opportunity for her to create her own country and set all her own rules, but she didn't want her own country. All she was interested in creating was a little village on the sea with a circle of houses. Next, I told her to write a declaration of what her little village stood for—of what it could offer to humanity—which may make our modern world a better place. Her response was that we should "make a place for people to understand our relationship with Mother Nature and how she helped us to grow and thrive." She said this place would be for everyone—people who are "lost" or "homeless" as well as for anyone who just wanted to be close to nature.

In her vision, one of the rules of the society is that you can eat meat only on Thursdays, to teach the preciousness of all life. Another is that you can use "technology" only for one hour per day, and if you need to speak with someone, you will need to walk around the village and find them rather than calling or texting them. Perhaps my favorite part of her little village were the regular activities whose purpose was to provide an opportunity for people to enjoy and reflect on their connection to nature. She suggested things like musical performances, festivals, and scientific talks about the ecosystem. She also proclaimed her desire to encourage residents to do little things like watch sunsets, take walks, and reflect on their experiences through poems, songs, and drawings. Her hope was that being close to nature and taking the time to consider the role of nature in their lives would help people to understand that "we didn't do it on our own." Without the sun, she said, her eyes gazing off into the distance as she spoke, at some unseen point, "we would not exist." She went on to say that we need to understand this connection "in our hearts" so that we can stop destroying the environment.

My nine-year-old student has a breathtakingly intimate understanding of the interconnection of humans with the natural world. If this understanding were universal, embraced by all adults, we would immediately do as Greta Thunberg urges: we would stop investing in fossil fuels and begin transforming our global energy and transportation systems. We would price things according to the cost of the products' entire life cycle, including toxins leached into the Earth, cost to diversity, and energy required to break things down into waste. We would stop subsidies for industries that are moving us in the wrong directions and offer incentives for industries trying to solve our climate problems. We would heavily regulate the use of chemicals and ban plastics. We would reduce meat consumption and make it much more difficult to cut down trees. We are so close now! In many parts of the world leaders really are beginning to talk about climate chaos with the gravity it deserves, even if it is not being taken as seriously as it should by all, and industry leaders are digging in their heels, denying their role in the catastrophe. There are people in positions of power who recognize the need for change; even if they don't have the votes to enact those changes now, their voices are being heard, and the conversation is being had. We are making *some* progress, but much, much more is needed. In a situation such as this, which affects everyone of us, it is important that we ask what we can do—as citizens, as educators—to bring us closer to the change we need.

To answer this question, consider the village that my nine-year-old student envisioned: *What does it have that we are missing?*

For me, the answer is obvious: *love.*

Love for humans and nonhumans alike.

To access and cultivate love in our lives is to cultivate inner peace.

From peace comes power: the power to envision change; the power to raise our voice; and the power to weather difficulty.

The greatest source of love we know comes from the energy that is around us always—in the spirit of the natural world; in the trees, oceans, mountains, and plains; in the interconnection of all living beings. Perhaps you find this as we (Amanda and Jing) do, in the energy of the natural world, or perhaps you call it by some other name: God, prana, or qi. Whatever name you give it, the concept of our interconnection with the spirit of the natural world is as old as the ages, recorded in some of our oldest spiritual traditions.

As you begin this chapter, we would like you to imagine that our most precious, essential gift as humans is wrapped up in, and interconnected with, the spirit of the natural world from which we came, and that it is our attempt to create a false separation between ourselves and that spirit, wrenching us so from the natural environment that we look upon it as an object—quick to disrespect and disregard—which has created the moral chasm we now find ourselves in.

Patricia Mische, author, academic, and professor, once said that "to try to separate nature from human nature, or to diminish the nature in human nature, is to wage war against our own essence."[1] If this is true, as we (Amanda and Jing) believe, then the powerful spirit of the natural world is within each of us already. She is a part of our "essence" just as much as we are a part of hers. As such, we have the very energy of life running through our bodies. To access it, we do not need to reinvent our lives. We do not need to reimagine ourselves as something other than what we are. Rather, all we need to do is open our hearts and learn to see with fully awakened eyes.

Perhaps it will help to quiet our minds with breath, smooth out the wrinkles in our perception, and let love bloom naturally. Through attention to the breath, in meditation or in prayer, we give ourselves a break from the constant interruption of the critical mind, and allow ourselves to feel the love that is around us always.

Let's rest here for a time, without anxiety, without the hollowness of false separation.

Jing: Major religions in the world urge people to love each other; they posit a fundamental force that creates all life forms and existence out of Love as a life-force energy that makes the Earth a living being. It is through contemplative practices, meditation being the major one, that many spiritual teachers came to open their heart to and align their spirit with Love as the penetrating consciousness and the highest moral order in the cosmos. We do have techniques and technologies to tap into the life-force of Love and embody it (Culham & Lin, 2020). A contemplative turn is required to centralize our learning for inter-being, for intuition, and tuning in with the cosmic consciousness embedded among all life forces, for a unity of consciousness.

Inspirational Stories from Fiction

In the fantastical world described by Shannon Messenger (2012–21) in her fiction book series for young adults "Keeper of Lost Cities" (recommended reading from my ten- and twelve-year-old nieces), there is an Elven world that exists alongside the human world, but in hiding. Why did the elves go into hiding and erase themselves from our human memories? Because we invented nuclear weapons and committed unspeakable acts of violence, a desecration of their commitment to peace and compassion so intense that they simply could not stomach being in contact with us (humans). So, the elves withdrew from our conscious awareness while continuing to monitor our "progress," doing what they could to mitigate our missteps before we caused too much catastrophic damage.

The elves are introduced as a peaceful species who pride themselves on creating a utopia-like world for their inhabitants. In this world no one has to worry about money (everyone is given, at birth, more money than they will ever be able to spend in their lives), which frees them up to do only what they love and removes the basic concerns of food and hunger. More important, however, for the purposes of our conversation, is the energy the elves put into living in balance with nature.

One of the things the elves do is secretly save all species of animals that humans drive to extinction and keep them in sanctuaries. In the sanctuaries they undergo rigorous training for their new life in the Elven word. This includes being taught to eat a vegetarian diet, like the elves themselves, who eat food naturally grown from plant products engineered to taste like meat but with an even greater nutritional value. The main character of the series is an elf who grew up in the human world, and so as a teenager she is discovering the Elven world for the first time. The first time she sees a dinosaur in an elven sanctuary (which is covered in neon feathers), one of the keepers explains: "We have colonies of everything. Mammoths, saber-tooth tigers, dinosaurs . . . Every species exists for a reason, and to allow one to die off would rob the planet of the unique beauty and qualities it provides. So we make sure they all continue to thrive."[2] Here we see that Messenger's reimagining of our relationship with animals is rooted in the same concept of interconnection between humans and the natural world that this book is addressing.

As silly as it may seem to be drawing on a fantasy novel at this point, I bring in Messenger's Elven utopia here (purposefully leaving out the problems the elves face) because sometimes, in searching for inspiration, it can be helpful to let ourselves sink into the magical world of fantasy, lingering for a time in what is *possible* rather than what *is*.

Jing: In the Confucian classic, the Book of Rites, Confucius
   envisions the future world to be fully equal and compassionate,

and everyone works for the good of All. A section in the Book of Rites states: "When the great Tao prevails in the world, the world is for the Good of All. Capable people are elected to govern; people trust each other and live in harmony; people are good not only to their family or children, they also take good care of the elderly people; adults have opportunities to use their abilities, children are well nurtured and grow well, and the widowed, handicapped and lonely people are all looked after. . . . There will be no hidden secrets, no stealing and no need to lock doors—this is the World for All." In Taoism in Tao Te Ching, Laozi declares: When the Great Tao prevails, the whole world works for the Good of All. Both Confucius and Laozi allude to the nature of human beings, which is part of the Tao, the creative, loving force that is unconditionally loving. Both teach that we need to live according to our true nature. When we do this, there may still be weapons, but they will be of no use.[3]

Suggested Reflective Activity #5: Opening to the Inspiration of Fantasy

As you respond to the reflective writing activity that follows, try to let go of the confines of the real world in which we live, letting the easiness of fantasy and the possibility of magic transport you to a place of pure imagination.

To prepare, find a quiet, comfortable place, and take some time to remember what it was like to be a child—to dream without limitation. To live in a world beyond what it is possible to see. Enjoy what it feels like to let go completely; wander, for a while, in the world of fantasy.

To get started, we invite you to FREE WRITE on any or all of the following questions:

What does my fantastical utopian world look like?

Or, if you find it more useful to write in response to prompts, consider finishing these sentences in your own words.

1. If I had the power to magically create a fantastical utopian world, the most important characteristics or qualities of that world would be . . .

2. In my fantastical utopian world, people would . . .
3. In my fantastical utopian world, people would *not* . . .
4. If I had the power to magically transform problems in today's world—without having to worry about opposition, financial constraints, or any of the limitations of our current reality—I would choose . . . because . . .

Inspirational Stories About Food: Meat-Free and Carbon-
Free Agriculture

Messenger's imagined Elven world, so committed to nonviolence that even animals are taught to eat vegetarian, is clearly a fantasy, but at the same time, humans do seem capable of almost anything—sending people to outer space, performing organ transplants, printing entire houses on 3-D printing machines. History has shown that if we are able to *imagine* a new way, and if we put enough resources behind it, we can accomplish what ten years before had seemed unthinkable . . . the stuff of fantasy.

Consider the agricultural industry. Estimates vary widely as to the exact percentage of total global emissions that the production of our food represents. The Food and Agricultural Administration of the United Nations puts the number at approximately 14.5 percent of total global emissions, while scientists at Stanford University have conducted a study that puts the number much higher, at nearly 68 percent, arguing that changing to a plant-based diet could cut emissions so quickly and to such an extent that it would give Earth's ecosystem the time it needs to phase out fossil fuels on a reasonable timeline.[4]

With the potential for such enormous gains, it is no wonder that private companies like *Blue Horizon* in Germany are investing in an "alternative protein market" and arguing loudly for other companies do the same. Similarly, NGOs in the United States, like The Good Food Institute, and private companies like Impossible Foods, are working on ways to revolutionize the food industry so that plant-based meat products will one day be a real possibility.[5] Most of these companies laud the development of a new, plant-based food production system aimed at satisfying meat-eaters with food that looks like meat, tastes like meat, and even provides our bodies with similar—if not better—benefits.

This science of plant-based food production is an offshoot of cellular agriculture. Without going too deeply into the science, cellular agriculture is the process of producing products from cell cultures. Cell cultures can start from living, or once living cells, like those taken directly from animals, or they can start with acellular material, like proteins and fats that do not contain living organisms. Scientists call this relatively new type of cellular agriculture "fermentation-based cellular agriculture," a term coined in 2015 by a scientist at a US-based company called New Harvest. It involves genetically modifying "bacteria, yeast or algae by adding recombinant DNA so that when they are fermented in sugars they produce organic molecules . . ."[6] These organic molecules can then be processed into products like milk or leather, which are, according to scientists, nearly biologically identical to the original.

Some companies already produce food products without the need of animals, such as milk and cheese. These can be made in laboratories using microbes (like yeast) and inserting them into pre-made cellular cultures creating what some scientists argue is, in fact, *milk*, the exact same as what comes from a cow, but without the need for industrial agriculture.[7] The Good Food Institute predict that cellular agriculture will be a burgeoning, new, sought-after profession one day among scientists, and that in ten years cultivated meats will be common in grocery stores and dinner tables (The Good Food Institute).[8]

Perhaps real competition for the meat industry, which can not only claim a nonviolent approach to producing meat products, but also claim a benefit for the planet, will lead to even more positive change in the way we raise and slaughter animals. Or perhaps it will put the industrialized food industry out of business altogether, helping us to make much needed changes in the way we live alongside animals. Regardless of what the future may hold, this story is a story of hope and human ingenuity. It shows that where we have problems, even those as enormously complex and important as feeding the world, we also have brave, dedicated people working toward solutions, proving once again that if we can imagine a better world we are one step closer to making it a reality.

Perhaps you are thinking to yourself—*that's great, but these companies are definitely motivated by the potential for future profits, which are made possible by our capitalist system*. To this, I would agree. Here, I want to reiterate that the purpose of this book is not to demonize any one system of belief, or any one story. Rather, our purpose is to clarify where we are now, ask questions, and consider ways to bring us *into balance* without the planet and its ecosystem. Balance does not mean throwing out what works and starting over from nothing. It means calling up what has been stomped out so that we can find our feet. It means remembering that we are not alone on this planet. That we share it with an entire ecosystem of animals, plants, and natural wonders, as well as other humans. We do not need to start over, but we do need to check if our current stories and processes are operating ethically, and where they are not, we need to work toward positive change.

Inspirational Stories of Grace and Spirit

Grace of God

Today I took a walk through my neighborhood and listened to a podcast from my brother's church. I am not a Christian, but I like to listen to my brother's pastor—it helps me feel closer to my brother, and I can find a universal truth in every sermon.

Today, the preacher mentioned the strength and power of the gospel, which is there for its followers to lean on. He said that we do not need to find the power on our own, we only need to open ourselves to the boundless, compassionate, loving energy of the Lord. For me, this concept of the eternal, boundless energy of the Lord seems deeply connected to the Taoist conception of *qi* energy: Taoists ask us to allow *qi* into our bodies to nourish, support, and guide us in our actions, just as Christians ask their followers to open themselves to God's boundless, loving energy. In both cases, the source is powerful and endless, a part and parcel of the complex universe that is, despite our advanced sciences, still an enigma in so many ways.

The preacher then spoke of Grace, or the unmerited, undeserved love and kindness bestowed upon every person by God, through which sins can be absolved. When you consider this act of Grace as a feeling—to be loved boundlessly by your Creator despite your sinful nature; to be forgiven and loved equally, as much as He loves every other living thing—it is almost impossible to comprehend. What does such boundless love feel like? When I go to church with my brother, I have often seen the feeling overwhelm worshippers who, as they lift their hearts in song, have tears of joy streaming down their faces. The feeling is so infectious that I find myself moved by proxy, the enormous possibility of such a love shaking something deep inside me.

Regardless of our background, faith, or spiritual tradition, unconditional love seems, to me, something we are all hoping and striving to discover. It is, perhaps, similar to the feeling of unconditional love some lucky children feel from their parents, people who protect and defend us as if we were one flesh. Whether or not we receive this kind of love from our families is not a choice we have control over, while finding this kind of love through faith or spirituality is possible for anyone who is able to open their heart and mind wide enough to let that powerful energy in.

Grace of Mother Nature

Just as a loving God offers humans a possible path to experiencing a boundless, generous love that depends on no human, so too does Mother Nature.

Have you ever taken a walk in a forest and returned feeling lighter? Somehow fuller and more at ease? Surely we have all gazed in wonder at a scene of natural beauty—whether the ocean, forest, or sky—and felt a sense of peace. Perhaps we have even let the energy of the natural world seep into our bodies, rippling through us like an ocean wave, spreading into every crevice. Perhaps we have felt it washing away stress, anxiety, and fear, and returned to our lives feeling more whole than we did in the beginning. As if simply being "away" from the stress of our human world, immersed in the calming energy of nature, has found a way to heal and deliver.

I don't think this experience is an uncommon one. Yet, there is great variety in the way we choose to understand and interpret these experiences. What is universal is that the natural world does not judge or discriminate. She offers only acceptance, beauty, peace, and calm. She offers healing energy and places to breathe in the quiet we yearn for, yet struggle to find in our busy lives. But some of us remain centered in our minds, sure that it is the act of "getting away" that is refreshing, not specifically the natural world, or the energy of the spirit. Others see it as a "coming home," a way to *rediscover* and *recenter*. This may seem immaterial, but as this book is hopefully making clear, the stories we tell about our experiences are the interpretive tools through which we create possibility. The stories we tell might activate those experiences into the cultivation of power, inspiration, and strength; or diminish those experiences, letting them quickly fade.

For hundreds of years writers, activists, religious leaders, and thinkers of all kinds have been pointing to the deep wisdom and healing power of nature. Both Thoreau (1862) and Lankford (1997) hint at the tendency of the "civilized" human to be so removed from nature that we misunderstand our relationship to it, perhaps even being so tricked or misled by societies' overwhelming tendency to "package nature" and distribute her as a series of products for our convenience that we come to see her as a resource rather than a loving companion, a source of spiritual connection and strength.

This conception of nature as something we can package for human consumption—into to-go containers, cuts of beef wrapped in saran wrap over Styrofoam, even the squares of grass bounded by sidewalks—is underscored by Lankford (1997), who reflects that "we think of food as something that comes from supermarkets rather than from the earth," and "[w]e think that water comes from faucets rather than from rivers and streams," just as we avoid thinking of meat as magically appearing in stores rather than as products of an industrialized process.[9]

How do we learn to reframe the Natural World as it really is?
To hold her lessons in our bodies?

Being Led by Nature

Thoreau made the case in his essay, "Walking" (1862), that in order to preserve his health and spirit it was necessary to spend at least four hours a day "sauntering through the woods and over the hills and fields, absolutely free from all worldly engagements."[10] Similarly, Emerson (1844) wrote that simply walking through a forest can persuade us to "quit our life of solemn trifles" and find peace, poetically describing a walk through nature as an experience of being absorbed into Her being, our senses overtaken "by new pictures and by thoughts fast succeeding each other, until by degrees the recollection of home [is] crowded out of the mind, all memory obliterated by the tyranny of the present," allowing us, at long last, to be "led in triumph by nature."[11]

This idea of being *led by* nature—allowing it to squeeze out conscious thought and lead us forward in a place outside of thinking—is a profound one worth pausing over.

Stories of Being Led

One way I (Amanda) have experienced nature *leading me* is in the times when I open myself to the wisdom of the forests, oceans, and mountains without judgment or criticism. For me, this happens when I surround myself in a natural environment, away from the business of the human world, and turn my attention outward. I open my heart and mind; I listen and breathe; and I wait for the natural world to speak to me. Sometimes I even ask, quietly—*what is it you want to say?* This often leads to a kind of knowing, or a particular piece of wisdom, sometimes clear enough to come in words, like a message.

For example, once in January of 2020 I traveled to Hawaii from Beijing to visit my brother and his family for the Chinese New Year. I planned to stay for two weeks, but within five days of my landing in Honolulu, the coronavirus was discovered in Wuhan, China. My brother invited me to stay until things cleared up—it was the logical thing to do given the pandemic—but I desperately wanted to go back to my life, which I felt was just getting started. I had a job there that I loved, an apartment, a fabulous literary community, and a group of friends I was excited to get to know better. This was before it became clear that the virus would spread very quickly or become very deadly, so whether or not I would return seemed like a question worth considering.

My flight home was quickly approaching; I needed to decide, but there were so many unknowns it was difficult to settle on anything. I was wrestling with the feeling of being so far away from my life and what felt, at the time, like my purpose, all of which was back in Beijing. I was also worried about staying with my brother, who over the last two decades I had seen only occasionally—on holidays, birthdays, and anniversaries. I wasn't sure if we would get along over an extended period of time, and despite enjoying spending quality time with him, my sister-in-law, and my four nieces, I worried I would be a burden—they were six people in a three-bedroom house, and I knew I would present a significant change in their daily lives.

One day I went hiking. As I walked, I emptied my mind. Like Emerson, I let myself be swept away by my surroundings. I turned off my thinking mind, and let myself be *led by* the path, my eyes darting here and there, pulled spontaneously. Suddenly, I stopped dead in my tracks at the sight of a tree, which stood tall and alone in a sea of grass and small bushes on the downward slope of a mountain. It was bold- and determined-looking. A strong, green, pine-needled thing that seemed to be standing its ground amid the chaos of bramble and bush, far from the other trees. Somehow, it commanded my attention, and so I stared at the tree for a long time, feeling—without thinking—that there was something I needed to learn from it . . . something it wanted to tell me. I felt a kinship with it, a closeness, and I did not want to leave.

I cannot say how long I stood and looked at the tree, but eventually I heard it speak: *be strong and plant your feet.* That is what it told me. I knew then, without question, that I had to stop yearning for my life in Beijing and stay in Hawaii.

I had no way of knowing then that this would not be a matter of just a few more weeks. Due to Covid, I would be there for four months, including over a month in full lockdown with my brother and his family. Had I been able to see this as a possibility, I might have run the other way. Instead, because of my fateful decision, the next four months became some of the most inspirational, beautiful months of my life.

I was integrated fully into the lives of my brother and his family—we took walks in the afternoon, ate dinner together each night, sat together each morning and evening, and attended church together every Sunday. As a spiritual atheist, I had a chance to experience my brother's religion (Christianity) with new eyes, seeing the positive messages of the preacher, and the ways it had helped them to shape their family through the values of love, kindness, and generosity. Through this experience I came to understand and respect his faith, where before there had been misunderstanding. In learning to respect and honor my brother's faith, I was able to create space for a strong and loving relationship which, prior to my time in Hawaii, had been strained.

Spending significant time with anyone creates the possibility for connection and love, and so it is no surprise that I was also able to form a close bond with my sister-in-law and my nieces. Together, my sister-in-law and I made grocery lists and went shopping each week, braving the crowds with our masks and disinfectant, while my nieces walked alongside me on family hikes, chatting about their hobbies and interests. I even read some of the books they recommended, leading to excited conversations between us about our favorite characters and moments. By the time I finally booked my tickets and prepared to board the plane back to the mainland, I had become part of their family in a way that had previously been unimaginable. When I walked out of their door and into my friend's car, every one of us was crying. If I had not had the clarity of mind I found on that mountain, if I had not allowed the spirit of the natural environment to ripple through me and speak, would I have stayed? Or if I had stayed for some other reason, would I have done so with the same degree of openness and inner peace?

> **Jing:** Indeed, in many religions and spiritual traditions, there is the notion that the world lives in us and we in it. We are part of everything. When we have a tranquil and humble heart, and when we are willing to listen, we literally hear nature. It can be felt in the body, experienced in the senses, as a feeling swelling in the heart, or as a whisper in the ear. We can communicate with our emotions. When we have so much love for each other, peace will prevail among all species. What Isaiah (Isaiah 65:25 and 11:6–7) predicts is possible: "The wolf and the lamb

shall feed together, the lion shall eat straw like the ox; but the serpent—its food shall be dust!"; "The wolf shall live with the lamb, the leopard shall lie down with the kid, the calf and the lion and the fatling together, and a little child shall lead them."

In my view, if we connect with each other heart to heart, the energy of Love pulsating in all existence can create magic like that described by Isaiah. But only if we center our education as a learning and embodying of Love for all species!

Suggested Reflective Activity #6: Exploring Our Relationship with "Spirit"

We invite you to FREE WRITE on any or all of the following questions:

1. How would you describe your relationship with spirituality?

   a. If you **do not** have a relationship with spirituality, what keeps you from it? Where do you find your power and strength?
   b. If you do have a relationship with spirituality, what name do you give it? And what practice, if any, do you have?

2. Do you have any personal stories to tell about the powerful energy of the natural world in your life?

   a. Is there a significant experience you can remember where the natural world brought you a sense of healing or peace?
   b. Have you have felt that wisdom has come to you, as it came to me that day on the mountain in Hawaii, from an unexpected, or unknown place?

      i. If so, what was the message? How did it turn out?
      ii. If not, what do you think about this experience?

Scene 5

PREPARATION
TOOLS FOR ACCESSING INNER WISDOM AND LOVE

Native American holy man and activist Lame Deer has said that "being a living part of the earth, we cannot harm any part of her without hurting ourselves."[1] If this is true, then each meat-processing plant, oil field, coal mine, and piece of plastic thrown in the ocean doesn't just harm the natural world, but it also degrades and erodes our collective human spirit. If we consider where we are today—with industry leaders and politicians struggling to find the motivation to do what is necessary to save our planet, not to mention all the life, human and nonhuman, which relies on it—the concept of a degraded spiritual being isn't so hard to imagine. If we are on a quest to rediscover our spiritual wholeness and heal from the past, then we will need spiritual tools to guide us. As you consider the spiritual tools and teachings presented in Scene 5, please keep in mind that we offer these up because of their great usefulness for us (Amanda and Jing). As the Buddha's Parable of the Raft teaches, spiritual tools exist to help us advance from point A to point B; as such, we do not suggest that these tools should supersede or replace your own faith.[2] So, if you have a strong faith tradition of your own, we encourage you to read this section for inspiration, then consider ways that your own faith may offer the same kind of guidance and hope for a future of spiritual wholeness that includes all living things. Once you find this guidance, we encourage you to share it with your own faith community.

> **Jing:** Spiritual awakening is the hallmark of gaining a sense of equanimity. The Buddha, through his awakening, sensed that humans cling to materials that are not permanent, and that ignorance led to a lack of wisdom about the multiple dimensions of life, as well as our inherent equality as living being, and the fact that we have lived as various kinds of species. We are kin to each other. In one lifetime he grew so much compassion for all living beings, together with a great sense of equanimity, that he

gave his life to feed six tigers.[3] Hence in Buddhism, compassion for all existence grows out of the embodied experience of our Oneness; once our Oneness is truly felt, it becomes natural to help others, as to do so feels the same as helping oneself.

On Meditation

At its core, meditation is a tool for gaining awareness of our thinking mind and opening our hearts to experience the creative energy alive in all existence—what some may call God, and which other major religions have called by various names, including *qi, prana, Ki, ruach,* and so on. As we gain awareness of our thinking mind and learn to separate ourselves from the constant chatter of our daily lives—often experienced as a running commentary delivered by an anxiety-ridden internal narrator—we in turn gain new sight, which allows our spiritual, bodily, emotional, and psychological beings to come into focus.

Most beginning meditators are overwhelmed by how difficult it can be to quiet the mind, and gain control over the constant chatter that follows us throughout the day. But with practice the mind calms, and what lies beyond or around the mind comes slowly into focus. We begin to glimpse the larger universe of energy that is always around us, stable, strong, and calm. We learn to identify sources of great power, such as the boundless love of nature and the interconnectedness of all living beings. While in meditation we are able to tap into these pools of strength, allowing them to fortify our bodies and relax our minds. We are able to cultivate kindness and gratitude for all we have, and to stop looking outward, beyond the present moment, for meaning. In essence, what we cultivate is a heightened awareness of who we are, recognizing that we are not the thinking mind alone; we are also the peaceful observer, and the vibrating energy always around us. As we learn to slip between these worlds, we may find ourselves buoyed upward until we are almost weightless, alive with love, warmed through with peace.

> **Jing:** Through meditation, I have had the profound and transformative experience of feeling the entire universe—the air, rocks, water, trees, and so forth—as alive and singing. I see all existence as engaged in a cosmic Song of Love, each manifesting their unique expression of this Love. I attributed this opening up of my senses to feeling the cosmic-ubuntu to meditation, through which I am in touch with the life energy

of all existence. This life energy, called qi or prana, is, in fact, consciousness and spirit. We live in a living world, a living universe. Our consciousness does not come from the brain, but from tuning into the universal consciousness that is in all existence.

Meditation and Nature

I once went to a yoga retreat with a group of friends and followed them to a Vision Walk Meditation being held in the nearby forest, beneath a canopy of trees. The meditation leader had us sitting around on tree stumps and chairs and closing our eyes as he led us through a meditation that asked us to sink deep into our heart chambers, quiet our minds, and release a question into the universe. Once we released our questions, we were told to open our eyes and let our intuition guide us to an answer. If we felt moved to perform our "vision walk" as a walk through nature, being literally led forward in a meditative state with Nature as our guide, we were to get up and follow our feet. However, if we felt moved to stay seated with our eyes open, allowing them to sweep across the natural landscape, or to remain in closed-eyed meditation, that was also encouraged. Whatever we felt called to do, our main objective was to remain deep in our meditative state, completely open to the wisdom of the universe, waiting for an answer. We were told that when the answer came it would be clear and direct, and we would know it immediately.

I wanted to know what I should do about a book I was writing. I felt stuck with the storyline and was unsure how to proceed, and so I asked: *What do I need to do to move forward with my writing?* With that question released into the universe I stood up, and walked along a dry dirt path, meandering silently in my meditative state until I came to a large succulent. It had one central root planted in the ground, around which a flowering of thick leaves sprouted in shining green handfuls. I stopped before it suddenly, as if directed by an invisible force, and stared, entranced. Almost immediately, as clearly as if the succulent had spoken in its own voice, I heard my answer—*map it out! Map out the story!* I shared my experience with the group upon returning, and when I went home that night I wrote my first reverse outline, finally getting a hold on where I was, and where I was going.

Before I left the yoga retreat, the workshop leader who had heard my story gifted me his book: *Vision Walk* (2006), by Brandt Morgan.

The book explains what a vision walk is, and provides the vision walk meditation that we engaged in that day in the forest. Since that day, I have done his meditation on my own innumerable times, as well as led groups of people through the vision walk experience, always with the same positive results. Personally, I have found that as long as I am in a deep meditative state, giving the question my full attention, I will receive an answer that is direct and true, even if it doesn't seem perfectly obvious to me at the time. I have also learned to trust what Brandt explains in the book: that we should not judge or second-guess the answer we are given, no matter how small or surprising the format it is given in might be.

For example, I once sat on a bench and asked what I should do next in my life. My eyes darted from the children playing among the tulips to the dogs walking past and suddenly my neck bent and I was drawn to the unmistakable sight of an airplane zooming by. The message was clear: travel. This seemed unreasonable at the time—I was in a relationship, living with my boyfriend, and deeply invested in a doctoral program. Nonetheless, six months later I had taken a job in Beijing and was starting a new life.

Another example was a question about the boyfriend I just mentioned, asked nearly a year before the fateful airplane sighting. In this meditation I asked the universe what I should do, and my eyes were drawn with a prophetic kind of force to a STOP sign. It wasn't what I wanted to hear, and obviously I did not listen right away, but a year or so later I finally came to terms with what I knew all along and ended things.

The book warns that this kind of hesitancy will happen, and explains that the most difficult part is not receiving the answer, but having the faith and self-discipline to listen, because often the answer feels out of alignment with our current life. This is because we are already living within "elaborate structures—complicated identities based on beliefs accumulated and practiced over many years" which serve as "the building blocks for who we think we are," while the answers that come to us through the vision walk "know no structures or boundaries."[4] They arise from the heart.

Through the practice of the Vision Walk meditation I came to feel that my intuition, which I understand as the wisdom of my inner being, could be linked with nature in powerful and straightforward ways. Over time, I learned that I could hear my own inner wisdom more clearly— even that wisdom I hid from myself—by letting the natural world speak. For me, this link between the natural world and my deepest inner wisdom has, over time and with practice, come to feel like a natural state. When I relax into meditation and open myself, I *will* be guided, quite naturally, to the wisdom I need.

> **Jing**: I fully understand that state of being Amanda described. Since I embarked on my journey of meditation over two decades ago, I know that I have all the answers within me. If I have a question, I would meditate and enter a tranquil state, and the answer would come up into my heart; sometimes I ask for insights from higher teachers and the response comes as an inner voice, or a paragraph I happened to read, or someone saying something casually. It seems the universe is intelligently wired, a heart with reverberating chambers, and we are all in the vibrating field resonating with each other's inner voice. What is key is to heed the voice, and as Amanda says, to trust it.

Accessing the Power of Meditation in Your Life

Sometimes in the daily machinations and routines of my life—walking to work or sitting at my desk—I suddenly see the visual and experiential planes shift around me, as if there is so much more to sense than what I am currently allowing. I can control and deepen this if I take a moment and breathe, or if I allow myself simply to slip in more deeply. I suddenly see the world as all of us who take the time will eventually: as hidden in plain sight, where colors are more vivid and the wind whispers and there is a felt energy to all things, including stones, people, concrete, pieces of fluff floating through the air from cottonwood trees . . . an energy that we merely need to *allow* in and it will spring to life in our bodies.

Those of us who meditate know that when we close our eyes and let the natural world speak, we are met with an overwhelming response: love, along with an abundance of gratitude and positive energy. I believe the same experience can be found in prayer, creating or appreciating art, as in tranquil moments by the sea. Perhaps you have had an awe-inspiring experience while snorkeling in crystal-clear water, watching the fish playing in the current, darting toward you and away. Or perhaps you feel an intense sense of peace when you watch the sunrise, or in singing as you swing back and forth in a hammock on a lazy summer's day. The magic of meditation is not found only during traditional meditation; rather, it can be found in a variety of ways, by entering a deeply aware, thoughtful state where we quiet our inner mind and let the rest of the universe (or God, or qi, or prana, and so forth) speak.

For me personally (Amanda), I have learned to listen to the wisdom of the natural world when I am in it. I know now that all I need to do is open my senses and surrender, letting the trees, or waves, or mountain trails lead and speak. This connection with nature can be felt anywhere—I have felt it in parks in the middle of the city, in a broken branch floating in the stagnant water of a fountain that had been turned off for winter, and in the rustling leaves of a sapling planted in a sidewalk, its branches reaching down like a blessing.

Listening to the wisdom of the spirit, however we name or envision its voice, is something that is possible for anyone, anytime, anyplace. When we let our edges soften and the rigid definitions of our selves blend into the larger world, we open up the possibility for wisdom to slip from that world into our conscious being. The wisdom we find is just as much a reflection of the natural world as the natural world is a reflection of our spiritual beings; it is the connection that matters, not one or the other individual thing.

I wonder if you, dear reader, have experienced it? The whispers that dance on your skin when you are near the quiet calm of an open field or the crashing waves of the ocean. For me it is a constant state; once the heart, mind, and ears are open—which can be achieved through meditation and a modicum of faith—it is something you can always come back to, indefinitely, over and over. For me this experience is so quotidian that I have trouble believing it is not experienced, on some level, by every human.

How is it for you?

How was it for the first imperialists who traveled across the oceans? Under the brightest stars, without another boat for leagues around them. Were they in awe of the sky and the endless water, even as they were tossed around at the mercy of its storms?

How was it for their soldiers?

Jing: Daoism believes that we are in nature and nature is in us.
There is an inner dimension that is as vivid as the outside
world, and this inner dimension connects with all life forces.
The pathway to peel through the outer layer of the world and
peek into the inner, deepest dimension of the reality is through
meditation, and following the way of Dao, which is to live for
the Good of All. In Traditional Chinese Medicine (TCM),
meditation opens the internal energy channel to connect us with

everything. Li Shizhen (1518–93), a TCM doctor and famous author living during the Ming Dynasty in China, wrote that he "opened up the inner channels of the human body and felt and resonated with all things" through meditation. From then on he saw another dimension of the human body, our energy body, flowing with qi in the meridians and acupoints, and he studied and documented how various elements in nature, such as herbs and minerals, are energies that can be used to balance the yin and yang energy flowing in our various organs and body parts.[5]

I (Jing) have had many experiences like Amanda's. When walking I see flowers having their distinct personalities and spirit, jumping out to me and expressing themselves, as do plants, rivers, mountains, not to say animals. I have encountered many animals that sense my love for them and instead of running away, look up at me and communicate with me through their eyes, tails, and ears. I even sense rocks and electric poles or a cup having their spirit, and even cities have distinct energies . . . All have qi and have spirit, energy, matter, and intelligence!

Suggested Reflective Activity #7: The Power of Spiritual Energy in Your Life

We invite you to FREE WRITE on any or all of the following questions:

1. What brings you energy and light?
2. What's the role of meditation or prayer—if any—in your life?

   a. If it has a central role, please tell a story where prayer or meditation has offered you guidance.
   b. If it does not play a role, can you tell a story of another way you have received guidance at a difficult point in your life?

3. If meditation or prayer is not present, what do you think you might gain from these tools given what has been shared in this chapter?

Yin/Yang and Feminine/Masculine

Feminist scholars and activists connect the mind-body split and devaluation of nature discussed in Act 1 to a devaluation of the feminine.

Women have, throughout history, been thought of as connected with *nature* and *emotion* while men have been stereotypically considered *strong minded*, *logical*, and *clear-headed*. Women were expected to take up reading, art, and music, while men took on business and politics. This conception of women as *emotional* and *closer to nature*—perhaps because of our ability to reproduce, or because of our nurturing, caring dispositions—has been used for centuries to support patriarchal structures, which claim that such dispositions are not suited to civic participation.[6] Over this enormously long stretch of human history, the natural balance of these two energies (male and female, feminine and masculine), and their concomitant ways of knowing, was disrupted.

The ancient Chinese concept of *yin-yang* energy holds that what is needed in the world is a balance of all energies. *Yin* energy represents the traditionally feminine values of nourishing, loving, sustaining, and harmonizing. *Yang* energy represents the comparatively masculine values of creating and motivating.[7] In the well-known symbol of *yin* and *yang*, these two types of energy are side by side, creating a circle that represents a complement of both energies. The energies are simultaneously working together to create a whole, and yet remain entirely distinct. This is why, when you look at the symbol, you will see there is a small dot of *yin* in *yang*, and a small dot of *yang* in *yin*; because despite being the opposite of one another, they embrace and enhance each another, so that *yang* is forever embodied in *yin,* and *yin* in *yang.* . Being in harmony with that which is different from you means understanding and embracing difference as strength; understanding that what seems in opposition may actually be what we need most. But throughout human history there has been a tendency to reject difference rather than embrace it, with many going so far as to isolate and demonize those seen as "other." Rather than learning from and celebrating "the other," we often choose to meet "the other" with rejection and shame, which often extends to suspicion, oppression, and control.

One essential difference among humans that has played an enormous role in our shared history is the difference between (the traditional conception of) the sexes: male and female. It is common knowledge that most societies around the world have traditionally privileged men over women and idealized male traits while relegating female traits to a lesser status. Additionally, most societies insisted that men and women are static and distinct, leading to a distilling of male and female into falsely singular beings. As the physicist and ecologist Fritjof Capra remarks, "[t]his attitude has resulted in an over-emphasis of all the yang—or male—aspects of human nature," including things like "activity, rational thinking, competition, [and] aggressiveness," while simultaneously de-emphasizing and oppressing those traits that are traditionally female, such as intuition, emotion, compassion, and spirituality.[8]

It may be that this domination of male traits in human society has led to many of the exploitative systems and structures of power we see today. In a world where privilege and status have been passed down to traditionally "male" men, the supposedly "male" traits of "activity, rational thinking, competition, [and] aggressiveness" have been lauded and idealized, leading to an overemphasis of these traits in our leaders, and therefore our societal norms and structures. Consider, for example, that since the advent of the merchant class in the seventeenth century, economic structures which favor aggressive competition have defined our global order, and by proxy, our international relationships. We measure our value and worth through the lens of competition, continually comparing ourselves to others: Who has the most wealth? Military might? Or international influence? In fact, it doesn't seem like a stretch to view today's global markets as ordered around *yang* energy: who can win the most power, sell the most desirable resources, or stare down an opponent successfully? In pure *yang* energy, whoever is the strongest, the loudest, and the best fighter will be celebrated and feared by others, while those attempting to operate according to pure *yin* energy (which imagines a completely different set of values) will be easily dominated. It may be that our thirst for the accumulation of wealth and power is spurred on by unchecked *yang* energy which, when left unchecked and out of balance with its opposing *yin* energy, is incapable of finding the balance it needs.

While today's modern world may be severely out of balance, with *yang* operating unchecked by *yin,* all is not lost from the Taoist perspective, which retains that no matter how hard we work to squeeze out *yin* and operate fully in *yang,* the essential nature of the universe's energy is balance. As such, the actual balance of *yin* and *yang* is always around us: it is our natural state. Taoists call the creative energy of the universe "qi," and maintain that despite which elements of this energy we choose to focus on as a society, this essence of *qi* energy cannot be distorted. Not in the universe, in nature, or in ourselves. While *qi* itself cannot be distorted, however, the way we cultivate, accept, and channel this energy is our choice. In believing that *male* and *female* energies are distinct and separate, or that one is inferior and the other superior, we cultivate an energy state for ourselves that is out of balance. We offer the Taoist conception of *yin* and *yang* as a way to understand our current crisis, and through that understanding, offer a challenge. The diagnosis is this: we are out of balance, and rediscovering our natural state of balance—first in our thinking and feeling, then within our societal structures and governing bodies—is necessary to combat climate change. The challenge is to find a way to cultivate a balance of *male* and *female* energy, which includes a balance of mind with body, logic with intuition, and science with spirituality. If we were to rediscover this balance in ourselves first, learning to pull from *all* aspects of qi energy and operate as a whole, unbroken system, with the logical *yang* energy being cupped and nourished by *yin*, and the loving *yin* energy motivated and brought to fruition by *yang*, perhaps we would be able to create a "balanced condition that allows growth and restoration, exchanges and creation," ultimately pushing us forward as a whole, unbroken being.

We Inter-Are

The Buddhist scholar Thich Nhat Hanh describes our connection with the natural world as a full and complete state of *inter-being* where, by design, we *inter-are* with every living thing. He explains this concept in the opening chapter of his book "The Heart of Understanding":

> "If you are a poet, you will see clearly that there is a cloud floating in this sheet of paper. Without a cloud, there will be no rain; without rain, the trees cannot grow; and without trees, we cannot make paper. The cloud is essential for the paper to exist. If the cloud is not here, the sheet of paper cannot be here either. So we can say that cloud and the paper inter-are . . .
>
> If we look into the sheet of paper even more deeply, we can see the sunshine in it. If the sunshine is not there, the forest cannot grow. In fact, nothing can grow. Even we cannot grow without sunshine. And so, we know that the sunshine is also in this sheet of paper. The paper and the sunshine inter-are. And if we continue to look, we can see the logger who cut the tree . . . And we can see the wheat. We know that the logger cannot exist without his daily bread and therefore the wheat that became his bread is also in this sheet of paper. And the logger's father and mother are in it too. When we look in this way, we see that without all of these things, this sheet of paper cannot exist.
>
> Looking even more deeply, we can see we are in it too . . . Your mind is in here and mine is also. We can say that everything is in

here with this sheet of paper. You cannot point out one thing that is not here—time, space, the earth, the rain, the minerals in the soil, the sunshine, the cloud, the river, the heat. Everything co-exists with this sheet of paper . . . You cannot just be by yourself alone. You have to inter-be with every other thing. This sheet of paper is because everything else is . . . As thin as this sheet of paper is, it contains everything in the universe in it."[9]

Thich Nhat Hahn's passage invokes an image of the cycle of life through which we can see an order in things: clouds bring rain to a forest, which nourishes the trees that provide the paper we use to pass knowledge from hand to hand. From the sun comes boundless energy. Through its warmth we have the bounty of the Earth, without which you would not have this book in your hand or the ink on this paper. The very reading of these ideas is impossible without the sun and the trees, and so yes, a cloud exists in this piece of paper, just as the sun and rain are always present in every physical thing. This is *inter-being*—an interconnection between all living things which together create a deeply interdependent, interwoven field of shared energy. In this shared ecosystem, as Hahn writes, "you cannot just be by yourself alone. You have to inter-be with every other thing."

You "are," I "am," and every living being "is," only because everything in the universe "is." This is quite a shift from Descartes' "I think therefore I am," which places our existence at the foot of our intellect. For Hahn, **we *are* because the universe *is*.** We *are* because of the sunshine and the rain, because of the blades of grass and the trees. It is the same for the stars, the air, and the animals who share this space. In other words, interconnection is not a choice, but a *state of being*.

Intellectually agreeing that we *inter-be* with other living things, perhaps because it is scientifically sound or logical, is not the same thing as *knowing* the truth of this in our bodies. *Agreeing* is an intellectual exercise while *knowing* is an embodied state. If we allow ourselves to *know* that all things are connected, with our *whole minds* and our *whole bodies*, certain truths rise to the surface naturally. One of these is that to abuse, mistreat, or in any way denigrate those beings with which we *inter-are* is to inflict pain and suffering on our own spiritual bodies. And not just us, but our children, and our children's children, and on and on, indefinitely, until it is stopped.

If we accept the connection we have with all other living beings, compassion and understanding extend naturally, and it becomes impossible to see any other way. We will know with our whole being that when we lay waste to the natural world, we are laying waste to our own beings. When we discard, pollute, diminish, or treat living things as less than the miracle they are, we in turn degrade and diminish our own existence. These destructive acts are terribly selfish ones, smoothed over at the edges by psychological and emotional numbness (as we argued in Act 1), which leads not only to the ravaging of the Earth and the mistreatment of animals but also to the unmooring of ourselves from our extended family. This willful degradation of living beings requires *of us*, and breeds *within us*, a callousness that over time erodes our capacity for love—both toward ourselves and others.

The callousness in our hearts that has eroded the love for one another we so desperately need can be seen in every corner of the world, at every stage of our history. Looking back, a clear link can be found between the otherization of our Earth and human rights, making the lesson of *inter-being* all the more real: when we otherize and denigrate the natural world, we otherize and oppress human beings. Those who carry out this otherization and oppression become numb to the spiritual balance they carry, learning over time to reside in a state of imbalance, which is rewarded by our global economic system.

Hahn's concept of "inter-being" is a powerful tool for envisioning the way that *how* we live is deeply interconnected with the state of our current crisis. If there is a cloud present in every piece of paper, then an imbalance in those clouds can lead to chaos in the system. As such, historical inequalities and the deeply rooted devaluation of nature is present in every drop of polluted water. To address this interlocking system of problems we need to change more than policy . . . we need to change our hearts and minds, so that as the right policies are turned into law, they are enforced and sustained with the righteousness of belief deeply felt in our hearts and whole beings. If human beings existed in a state of balance, which respected, loved, and honored all living beings, transforming our social structures so that they were organized around principles that valued *every* living being would occur naturally.

Suggested Reflective Activity #8:
Considering Yin, Yang, *and* Inter-being

Let's take some time now to reflect on the concepts of *yin* and *yang,* as well as *inter-being.* To get started, **we invite you to FREE WRITE on any or all of the following questions:**

PART A:

Finish the following sentences in your own words:

1. I experience the concept of *interconnection* when I . . .
2. I feel most "in balance" when . . .

PART B: yin/yang

3. How do you personally relate to the concept of male/female energy inside your own body?

    a. Would you describe yourself as in or out of balance? Why?
    b. Do you see reflections of this in society? If so, in what way?

4. What stories can you tell, from your personal experience, that showcase the imprint of **spiritual imbalance**?
5. What stories can you tell, from your personal experience, that showcase the healing power of **spiritual balance** or **spiritual power**?
6. If we were to seek better balance, how would we begin?

PART C: Inter-being

7. Does Hahn's concept of *inter-being* ring true to you?

    a. If so, in what ways?
    b. If not, why?

INTERLUDE

TWO STORIES

Andrew: The Creative Genius of a Businessman

Now, sit with me for a moment.
Get comfortable.
I want to tell you a story . . .

There once was a man named Andrew. Andrew was tall, blue-eyed, with a strong jaw, dark hair, and broad shoulders. He was raised by an artist and a lawyer, as the eldest of four brothers. Growing up in such a large house required Andrew to navigate personalities, vie for attention, and make arguments to get his way. Soon Andrew discovered that he had an impressive natural talent: he could look at a group of people and tell you who was feeling good, who was feeling on edge, why, and how to fix it. He knew how to read a room. Because of this, he spent a lot of time thinking about the way things worked and how they could work better. He realized he was particularly adept at understanding how to make things run smoothly and efficiently, as well as how to bring people along. Once he had an idea for how to improve something, he would be overtaken by a kind of whole-body passion to share that with others: he had a solution, and he wanted people to benefit from it.

Andrew had his first real taste of success in college when he noticed that his fellow classmates were a bit bored with the on-campus entertainment options. The idea came to him one night while sitting with his friends, throwing back a few beers, batting around ideas to help: he would rent buses and take the students to a new entertainment district each weekend. One bus grew to two, two grew to ten, and soon his business was such a success that it began draining funds from the university, which was used to making quite a bit of money off its students on the weekends. After a year of financial loss for the university, the university offered to buy Andrew out for one million dollars.

Andrew hadn't created his bussing system for the money; he did it because of how it felt to make something out of nothing. And because it felt good to identify a problem and offer a solution that made people around him happy. But one million dollars was a huge amount of money for a twenty-something, and he couldn't say no, so he took it.

The deal was a historic one for the university, and through it Andrew started getting a lot of attention. People told him he was a genius, and they wanted to know what he would do with his money. He saw that he was celebrated for his financial success and began to crave more of it. What would his next step be? How could he make the little he started with expand to something even bigger?

Andrew was the kind of person who could be good at anything . . . he understood how to cultivate good, strong relationships, grease wheels, and move mountains. In fact, he felt most alive when he was embarking on something new, and he felt energized by challenges, the bigger the better. He liked it when the proverbial mountain to climb was so high, the peak nearly impossible to see, that he had to start off guessing. The more complex the task and the more opaque the problem, the more excited he got about it. With this in mind, he began studying the market, reading about politics, and became interested in the Middle East . . . everybody in the world needed energy! And so Andrew took his million dollars and invested it in oil fields.

He lived for nearly a decade in Dubai where he made so much money off of dealings in oil and gas that he was able to start buying other people's businesses. As his fortune grew, so did his power and influence; but for Andrew, what mattered was not luxury or fame. It was the high he got from being innovative enough and creative enough to make something out of nothing. And because he is human, he also loved waking every morning and feeling, because of the success he surrounded himself with, that he was worthwhile and important.

He became addicted to making deals that had not been made before, and making them with such efficiency and at such a profit that everyone would wink and nod and pat him on the back and say, *"You've outdone yourself again!"*

Like all human beings, he yearned for people to appreciate what he'd accomplished. For people to look at him and think: *There's someone who knows how to do it!* And by "it" they would mean that thing everyone is always trying to accomplish—an exciting life, a good life, a life worth living—and deep down, because this is our culture, they would also mean *profit*.

By forty he had already built an empire of oil, hotels, and eventually, because the market became attractive, solar panels. Today, Andrew has risen to the top of what is considered "successful" in his country's culture: he is rich, he is powerful, he *owns and possesses* many things, and therefore he is an example for people to point to . . . he is a role model for their children.

He spends his days flying from country to country, talking on the phone, making deals, and moving money—he takes all his profits from one project and puts it in another to get that one started, then when that one is up and running, he does the same thing all over.

He still loves the thrill of the unknown, the little tingle of excitement he feels each time he discovers something new to invest in. Each little project is like a baby bird that he adores and nourishes and pours his attention into until it is ready to spread its wings. He loves the feeling of the chase . . . the feeling that there is something out there only he can do, which others may even say is impossible, but which he knows is only another puzzle to be solved, another riddle to be turned over and over.

When he finds something new, he gives it his full attention and remains rapt, fully immersed, *especially when* the odds are against him. His thirst for this is unquenchable.

Over time, Andrew's idea of "success" has morphed from something he yearned for to a state of being. He has become so saturated with the way success feels in his body that he has become numb to it, and so he has had to search harder and stretch himself further in order to find the same high he had the first time he rented a bus and piled his classmates onto it . . . nothing so small would satisfy him now. Satisfaction comes from foraging into the unknown, accomplishing what others haven't already.

One of the reasons Andrew has been successful is that he knows the value of relationships. He knows that without the people around him committing their time and energy, he would not have gotten to where he is today. In order for people to commit all their time and energy to his dreams, they need to like him. This is something he has always known innately; it is a gift, and he knows how to use it.

Andrew escapes into nature when he can. He exercises, he cares about art, he reads. He knows that his businesses have not been kind to the environment—he knows he has contributed an enormous about of CO_2 and other waste, but he does not spend too much time dwelling on this. It is the way of the world, and if it wasn't him, it would be someone else doing it.

For Andrew, the Earth feels like an abstract concept—it is a resource governed by the market, and once the market deems that oil and gas aren't worth it anymore, there will be another challenge. But until that day, he is just a businessman with a keen eye for seizing opportunity. He has been on this path for so long he can't imagine stopping.

> **Jing:** The story of Andrew reminds me of the financial market. Most men in the trading floors were frantically making calls, cutting deals, moving blocks, feeling on top of the world, patting each other on the shoulder to trade information, celebrating with a lavish party on a victory or a big catch, and setting the next even more ambitious goals—they all do this for "wealth," pouring their life energy and whole soul force into these acts while it never occurs to them that the oil they are manipulating for profit is Mother Nature's blood and bone marrow which is being drained up;that the water that is flowing in our blood is polluted as rivers become polluted, and countless water species are losing their life habitat and dying off; and animals that are traded and represented as meat "futures" are living, breathing intelligent beings . . . As success stories pile up, egos soar, and Mother Nature cries in excruciatingly deafening pain into dead ears!

Andrew's Untapped Potential

Andrew is, by all the world's traditional measures of a man, a great success. He has an enormous amount of inner strength and a desire to lead that has made him successful by the most quotidian of definitions. Like most of us, he has been taught, since birth, that if he wants to distinguish himself and prove his worth, he *must make money*. It is a common dream, after all, to have a house bigger than you need, cars that cost as much as some people's yearly salaries, even to "own" your own private island. It is no surprise, then, that Andrew—raised in a culture that values the accumulation of wealth and ownership—has oriented his professional life around these same values, as so many in this world have.

What if Andrew had been taught that to be *great* was to be reflective, wise, and compassionate?

What if he was taught that the highest value in life came from protecting the Earth? Or from learning how to love? Or from learning how to create more balance in the universe?

What if he was taught that being successful meant solving the world's greatest problems? Such as new ways to conserve the Earth's blessings and elevate the poor and voiceless among us?

And what if society rewarded him for these things in the same way that they reward building oil rigs and ocean trawling?

What kind of changes might a man like Andrew, with an innate drive to make something out of nothing, and a willful determination that refused to listen to naysayers, have been able to accomplish had he operated according to an Earth-centered value system?

Andrew *is* a great man.

He balances and leads fifteen different global companies. He spends his days creating something out of nothing. Cultivating impossible relationships. Brokering deals. Making an enormous impact on the world around him. He is a man of enormous courage, power, and energy. But because of what is considered "success," his energy and wisdom are focused on wealth accumulation, leading to potentially devastating consequences.

What Andrew's story teaches us is that our current value system doesn't just harm us and our Earth, it also misdirects and pollutes one of our most critical resources: human ingenuity. It takes people who have a stomach full of desire to accomplish great things and pushes them into a life of emptiness and greed, telling them that accumulating wealth and power is how they will achieve it.

Jing: It is clear that what we need to have is a new consciousness, an awakening of our heart to feel for nature and embrace the sacredness of all life forms. We need to open the eyes of the spirit to see the beauty and sacredness in all things. We need our heart to feel that we are a part of everything, to know that we are to be deeply grateful for the blessings we receive from nature, and from here we will grow humility and love for all, and we will want to share, not to exploit. We need to feel that it is inconceivable to harm others because that would mean harming ourselves. We need to have a new template for success and happiness.

A Story From Phnom Penh

I (Amanda) want to tell you a story about a trip I made to Phnom Penh in 2019 for my forty-first birthday. I went to meet a friend who lived a few hours north, in the much smaller city of Siem Reap. Since my friend, who made significantly less money than I did, was taking a long bus ride down on her own to meet me for my birthday, I decided to book and pay for the hotel as a treat. Unsure where I should book our stay, I asked for her advice, and she suggested I book it along the Mekong River. After some price comparisons I booked a suite with a small kitchenette and living room, steps from the river. It had a rooftop pool and free breakfast. When we arrived and went out for our first drink, we realized that the neighborhood along the river was not the same as my friend had remembered.

We didn't venture far from the hotel that first night because we wanted to get a feel for the neighborhood where we'd be staying. We walked just a few blocks from our hotel and sat down at a plastic table on the side of the road, which functioned as a kind of informal drinkery. It was dusk and the sun was just beginning to set behind the buildings. As we sat, sipping on a glass of white wine we had purchased inside, the metal garage doors across from us were rolled up to reveal a long line of beauty parlor-style swivel chairs positioned in front of mirrors. Bags of makeup were brought out, drawers opened to reveal piles of hair-styling equipment, and counters covered in gels and sprays. In a matter of minutes each empty chair was filled with women.

At first, I thought this open-air beauty shop was a place for excited young women hoping to make a good first impression, but soon the women who had been sitting in the swivel chairs getting their hair and makeup done began lining up along the street, jutting out their hips and cocking their heads as men drove up and down in cars and scooters to "get a girl" for the evening. My friend, more tuned in to the ways of Cambodia than I was, was the first to realize what was happening. She leaned forward, whispering in my ear the mistake we'd made: "We're in the Red-Light District."

It was my first time in a Red-Light District, so I have nothing to compare it to, but given the state of Cambodia, I imagine it is more extreme in its poverty than would be common in developed nations. The women were all ages, but the majority seemed to be in their early twenties. Along with the women were transvestites and transgender women in extravagant dresses chasing men down the street, pointing and shouting. But this was nothing compared to the children.

Over the three days we stayed in that hotel we began to notice a dedicated group of children who roamed the few blocks around our hotel freely, without any sign of a caregiver. One was a teenage girl, who looked no more than thirteen. She was tall and thin. Her long brown legs were bare in the hot summer wind. She wore what looked, in some ways, like a cheerleading outfit—there was a ruffled green skirt barely long enough to conceal her underwear and a tight green and white top opened suggestively at the beginning of her cleavage. Her painted toes were encased in cheap yellow flip-flops, and her dark hair was hanging free around her shoulders. Loose at her side was a purse in the shape of a teddy bear. She stood before us for a time, gazing up the street with her arms crossed, a look of bored acceptance visible in the upward tilt of her raised chin.

Another of these children was a boy, no more than three or four years of age, who ran actively back and forth across the street, up and down the sidewalks on both sides, in and out of parked cars and busy storefronts where he doubtless knew the workers. He was barefoot and bare-chested each of the two nights we saw him, and clearly acclimated to the life he was living. With his chest puffed out and his steps sure and resolute, he dodged his way through the crowd, hustling money from people. There always seemed to be a few paper dollars balled up in one of his hands, and a look of determination on his pursed lips. He somehow gave the surreal impression of being proud of his position: as if he owned the garbage-strewn street he roamed each night; as if finding people to swindle a dollar from was a coveted skill he had perfected over years of practice. I wondered if there was anyone waiting for him to come and hand over that money, or if he would use it himself to buy a piece of bread or a drink.

It was hard for us to take our eyes off of this child, and nearly impossible to reconcile his larger-than-life attitude with his age and size. The first time we saw him he was walking diagonally across the busy intersection after midnight as if it were his living room, the place where he was fed and cared for by whoever was around that evening. The second time I saw him he was by himself, standing in an abandoned tuk tuk that had been parked on the side of the road, staring out the window aimlessly. The third time was around one in the morning; my friend and I were having a late-night snack at the side of the road and he came and stood with his back to us, surveying the scene. His shoulder blades bulged as he reached one hand up mindlessly to touch a cloth banner advertising pizza for tourists. The other hand hung loose at his side with a rolled bill in his chubby fist and his shorts so low on his waist that the top of his butt was showing. I snapped a picture, because I didn't want to forget.

That night I sat on our balcony looking at the picture and cried—not just for him, but for the cycle of poverty and anger all around us, and the debasement of human dignity I was dipping in and out of so easily. These lives that exist and go on existing whether or not there is anyone from another world—a richer world, an easier world—around to see them.

I realized, after studying the picture carefully, that seeing him from the back was the best way to really imagine his age: without his puffed-out chest in full view, without his clamped lips or the daring smile in his eyes, it was easier to imagine the emptiness of care that led him to adopt such a persona. I was able to see who he might have been in a different place and a different time; but this was Phnom Penh in 2019, and it was the Red Light District. Being born here, to a mother who (if she's alive) probably needs to hustle her body to eat, offers little in the way of possibility. What are the chances that these children will become anything more than street-smart hustlers, pimps, or mistresses?

As we sat by the side of the road there was another young girl who came and sat at the table with us. She slumped angrily across from my friend with a scowl on her face, staring at my friend as she was eating. She was younger than the other girl we'd seen, no more than seven or eight, and clearly not selling herself—not yet, anyway. Instead, she carried a basket full of gum and put it wordlessly on the table in front of us without even bothering to ask for money. She looked at us with eyes that were exhausted and demoralized, too uninterested in the words or questions from my friend—who speaks a little Cambodian—to bother replying. She seemed, in that moment, to be a combination of angry, hopeless, and demoralized. It was so heartbreaking, and so completely *uncomfortable* to see.

I felt bad for taking her picture, but I wanted to remember what this felt like. I didn't want to get on the airplane and fly away and forget that look on her face, or the way it made me feel: at a loss, embarrassed, disgusted. Not just with the situation, but with myself . . . with the whole lot of us for allowing this to happen.

Getting back on the plane, in my comfortable clothes and nice shoes, looking out the window as Phnom Penh became a little dot below us, felt wrong. It felt, for lack of a better word, like a betrayal. I felt the impact of their faces slipping away as I put my seat back and gazed out the window. The disgust I'd felt being replaced by pangs of hunger in my belly. As soon as I was back in my apartment in Beijing, writing my first draft of this book, I had all but forgotten the rawness of that feeing. Writing it here, now, is one small offering I can make, and it is woefully insufficient.

There are many levels on which I see this story as an important addition to the discussion we are having about value systems and sustainability. One is the revealing way that the deprivation of human beings around the world seems to go hand in hand with a lack of care for the environment (as discussed in Act II). As I walked the streets of Phnom Penh, the coupling of poverty and disregard for the environment were palpable—people who are struggling don't have the capacity to care about such things. I snapped pictures while I was there of streets with mounds of garbage piled in the center, high enough to reach my knees. Over the years that my friend has lived there, she has sent me pictures of riverbanks covered with bottles and bags. None of this is likely surprising, yet it is important to draw out as a reminder to us all that a book about sustainability, which argues for a value system of compassion and love for all living creatures, is also—inextricably—a book about social justice.

If we cultivate an ethic of care and come to understand the world as truly interconnected, we will have no moral choice available to us other than to lift those in the margins of society out of poverty. It will be the work of a compassionate world to give every living being an equal chance at health and happiness as their counterparts in developed societies.[1]

Jing: It takes courage to make a change. However, if we learn to let go of the self, let go of the obsession with tangible reward, we will find that change is within reach, and it will be very genuine and in tune with our inner desire. For me, change started when I began to conceptualize this course and work with my students to educate each other about the power of vision and action; when I began to collaborate with scholars to write about environmental education and form groups to find collective strength for what we believe in. I also feel empowered by just saying hello to flowers and trees when I am walking, and saying thanks for the Sun, Moon, and Mother Earth every night. Remembering that our thoughts are vibrations that can travel to infinite space, that we can be a force of change right here at this moment. I once had this powerful experience realizing that our universe is propelled by a powerful energy, Unconditional Love, which made me realize that if we are loving unconditionally, we are already contributing to positive changes in the world.[2]

Suggested Reflective Activity #9: Value Systems and Social Justice

We invite you to FREE WRITE on any or all of the following questions:

PART A:

1. In what ways has the value system Andrew lives by arisen in your life?

- What about your friends? Family?
- If this value system is something you do your best to keep at bay, reflect here on ways that it still manages to wriggle into your consciousness, AND/OR your strategy for keeping it at bay.

2. Do you agree that a change in our societal value system would lead to businessmen like Andrew being able to channel their energy in loving, generous ways?

    - Why/why not?
    - Do you have any ideas or suggestions about how we might go about making this new set of values something to live by?

PART B:
Considering Amanda's experience in Phnom Penh . . .

3. What stories can you tell, from your personal experience, which showcase the overlap of social justice and ecological justice?
4. What stories can you tell from your personal experience about the way our outrage at issues of social injustice fades once they are no longer in front of us?

    - Why do you think this is so?
    - Do you have any suggestions about ways we might keep these experiences in the front of our mind?

Act III

FROM ROOT TO BRANCH: CONSIDER THE MYRIAD
WAYS WE LEARN TO BE

Scene 6

THREE INFLUENCES ON CHILDREN TODAY
FAMILY, ENVIRONMENT, AND SCREENS

1. Family

It is in childhood that belief systems and views of the world are first formed, based largely upon the ideas and norms presented to us by our primary influences. American psychologist Uri Bronfenbrenner offers a useful way of understanding this web of influences, which he calls our "microsystem," and describes as including our family, friends, school, neighborhood, religious affiliations, and other microcommunities we interact with as children.[1] Our parents, of course, often have the dominant influence because many of us spend the majority of our childhood with them nearby. They shape our home environment and are often the ones who take a first crack at explaining the world to us— what is right and wrong, and why. They are there when we confront difficulties, and they provide the best answers they can to our first big questions, giving us the material with which we'll form our first big ideas.

Whether our parents will have a positive or negative influence feels, in many cases, like the luck of the draw. Consider my uncle, a white man in his early seventies. As a child growing up in the 1960s, he was told by his mother that Black Americans had been systematically and terribly oppressed for hundreds of years and so he needed to be sensitive. His mother told him this with such solemnity and seriousness that, despite it happening half a century before, he remembers the way she looked when she said it. Would my uncle have become someone who is sensitive to racial injustice and aware of his white privilege, as he is today, arguing with many in his generation who do not believe in, let alone understand, the concept of institutional racism, had his mother not instilled in him an understanding of his own privilege at such a young age? Would he still have dated outside his race as he did, providing my first example of an interracial couple? On the other hand, consider my childhood friend whose family provided a different kind of influence. Her mother was an alcoholic and her father had trouble showing love to his children. Is it a surprise that she struggled with depression all her life, and eventually with addiction? Or that her relationships were volatile?

Despite the outsized influence of our parents on our disposition, as Bronfenbrenner explains, they are far from the only influence. Other parts of the microsystem into which we are born might shrink or expand our window of vision depending on their scope and variety. It matters, for example, if we go to a school with people who look like us, or if we have the opportunity to attend school in a diverse racial, religious, and cultural environment. Similarly, our window of influence might also expand if we like to read about other cultures and ideas. If we travel to foreign places or if we have the opportunity to form meaningful relationships with people outside our race, religion, socioeconomic status, and/or nationality. Research shows that if we have been exposed to, and form relationships with, people who are different from us, we are likely to be more accepting of differences.[2] Without influences on our ideas, experiences, and systems of belief that differ from our family unit, however, we may never question the worldview we were raised with, or the belief systems handed down to us as children.

For a great majority of us, the variety and scope of influences upon our worldview, which go a long way toward defining the way we understand ourselves and the world around us, are relatively narrow. This is because most of us stay, whether by choice or circumstance, in narrow lanes of race, class, and culture, exposed to an infinitesimally small number of ideas and philosophies (compared to the vast array of which exist in human history). We are often surrounded for the majority of our lives by just a handful of people who probably have similar experiences to us and agree with us on many things. But even exposure to new ideas doesn't mean we will definitely take those new ideas on, incorporating them into our worldview, allowing ourselves to grow and change.

One of the central themes of this book is that change requires bravery. Even if we grow up to be the kinds of people lucky enough, or determined enough, to expand our systems of influence through higher education, travel, or relationships, the extent to which we are willing to question, not to mention substantially *transform*, our belief systems, depends on our willingness to be uncomfortable—intellectually, emotionally, physically—and on the level of courage and patience we have for unraveling foundational systems of belief that have come to feel as real as the ground beneath our feet or the roof over our heads.

For myself (Amanda), the best example I can give is coming to terms with my privilege as a white woman raised in a middle-class, Christian family with access to higher education. At forty-two years old, I took a difficult dialogue course at the University of Maryland that required me to face the myriad of ways I have benefited from the systems of racial oppression which structure American society. Each week we looked at a different kind of privilege and oppression, and each week we (the students) were asked to turn the lens around to look at our role in the system. Doing that with openness and honesty was both embarrassing and scary! I went through a roller coaster of emotions—anger, denial, frustration, victimization, depression—but finally, through the guidance of my professor and the support of the students in the class, I came to a kind of understanding that I continue to engage with and work through today. Now that I've begun the work, I can't imagine returning to the white blindness I was living in previously.[3] Looking at ourselves clear-eyed and being willing to admit our faults and attend to much needed change isn't easy, but if we are open to being wrong, willing to listen, and determined to create a better world for all living creatures, the result will be well worth the journey.

2. Environment

I grew up in a three-bedroom brick rancher, on a cul-de-sac, which kept traffic to a minimum. The neighborhood was solidly middle-class and perfect for children, with a young family in nearly every house, giving my brother and me a horde of playmates. Our backyard was a square of grass and concrete buffeted by neighbors on all sides, separated by wire fences, but there were enough trees on the perimeter to drop a thick blanket of leaves in the backyard in fall, which my dad raked into enormous piles for us to jump in.

In my memory, these piles of leaves were several times larger than me, and soft as a warm fuzzy blanket. I can still feel my elation at wildly jumping into them, arms out, back arched, legs kicking. In summertime there were fireflies, which I would catch in my hands and wonder at through the slits between my fingers. Across the street, behind the houses, there was a stream that I waded through with the neighborhood kids, looking for crawfish and minnows, and long metal tunnels beneath an overpass which we called "the sewer." The neighborhood kids liked to dare each other to walk through from end to end, feeling that when we were inside the corrugated steel we were in another world entirely, hearing nothing but the trickle of water beneath our feet and the faraway roar of car engines.

At the end of our street and along the backs of the houses was a thin cover of trees which, to my childhood sensibilities, was a forest. By any measure there were enough trees for a child to get lost in, and so like the other kids in the neighborhood, I saw these trees as an escape from the world around us. A place away from the exhaust of the street and from my own house, where I had to clean up after myself and be careful not to break things.

At the opening to the trees was what we called "the big rock," named as such because it was an abnormally large black rock that greeted us every time we walked through the invisible screen between "the neighborhood" and "nature," which the cover of the trees came to represent. I sought it out when I was sad, stood on it in times of triumph, and staged a photo shoot on it with my best friend and a disposable camera when I found out I was moving. In my childhood imagination, this rock became a sort of touchstone for the forest. I envisioned it as a symbol of the forest's central nervous system, a kind of queen's seat that demanded respect

When I returned to my old neighborhood as an adult, it was a shock to realize how small these slivers of natural space really were compared to the outsized role they took in my life. We, meaning myself and the other children in the neighborhood, were drawn to them as if they had a kind of tide, feeling that when we were surrounded by trees or when we had our bare feet immersed in the clear waters of the stream, we were in another world entirely, miles from rules, requirements, and expectations. Now that I have grown up and shared my story with friends from around the world, each with a story of their own, I come to understand how privileged I was to grow up with even this small sliver of nature around me.

> **Jing**: I remember in my childhood, I roamed in the woods,
> splashed in the rainwater on the road, caught fireflies, and took
> my everyday nap among the roaring cicadas. My siblings and
> I were rarely home unless it was mealtime. We were always
> playing outside, and our parents never worried about us as there
> was no car to run us over, and every adult knew every child in
> the community. So we played until dark and until we felt hungry.
> I spent a lot of time when I was four or five years old carrying
> buckets of water to pour down little holes on the ground, and I
> felt literally lost in the act; time stopped and a huge peace filled

my heart until a little insect crawled out of the hole, which was wet and pooped in my hand as soon as I picked it up. I also caught fish with my hands. Moving into the future, which is now, many rivers in my hometown have dried up, and they turn into bright orange when it rains as red soils are washed into the river (over the years, mountains have been dug up to make bricks or leveled to make space for building restaurants and malls) and fish are no longer to be hand-caught anywhere. Most rivers are not safe to swim in anymore with all the toxins and pollutants in them.

These memories feel distant to me now, but I know they shaped me in essential ways. Perhaps being close to nature made it easier for me to recognize the power of nature in my adult life. Perhaps it even imbued me with a sense of calm in tumultuous times, or a deeper compassion for nonhuman beings. But today a childhood filled with play, let alone play that takes place in what's left of the wild spaces in our urban and suburban neighborhoods, is less common than ever. Our cities are expanding rapidly, causing suburbs to become more densely populated. The European Commission estimates that in 2015, 52 percent of the world lived in urban centers, 33 percent in urban clusters, and 15 percent in rural areas, making the total number of people worldwide living in an urban environment around 85 percent, or approximately 6.3 billion people whose children are having to look for nature in concrete-covered playgrounds or the green space of an urban park.[4]

In Beijing, green space is at a minimum, so children do their running around on concrete playgrounds or jungle gyms encased within the walls of gated communities. One of my Chinese students, a girl of nine who lives in Beijing's city center, has been kept indoors by her parents for almost a full month because they prefer her to study or play cello than wasting her time playing. When she does get to play, it is for scheduled periods— thirty minutes between the online classes she takes at home after school, or between working on her homework assignments. One of my youngest students, a six-year-old boy named Andy, arrives to our classes sweaty from playing outside with his friends, but their adventures are confined to the parking lot and the streets of his gated compound. They race up and down the little streets on their bikes, playing tag and looking for bugs crawling across the blacktop. It struck me, in talking to him, how he and his friends worked to find even the smallest natural thing and elevated it in their playful imaginations to something all-encompassing.

For people living in urban areas, crime may be a problem limiting access to play for children. My father grew up in Baltimore city in the 1950s and 1960s. When he was a child, parents let their children run freely through the alleys until dark; these days, such a thing would be a source of stress and anxiety for parents in Baltimore due to the high levels of crime. British writer and activist George Monbiot (2012) explains that "[s]ince the 1970s the area in which children may roam without supervision has decreased by almost 90%," indicating that a generation of children are growing up in a world very different than the one we (Amanda and Jing) grew up in as children.[5] In some countries there are other limiting factors, such as lack of sanitation and pollution; some estimate that among urban dwellers worldwide, one in three live in slum-like conditions, where children have little access to a clean natural environment, making the natural world unsafe, not to mention uncomfortable and unattractive.[6]

Jing: A few years ago, I was in China giving a lecture. I asked the students who attended the talk to name the beautiful things in their natural environment and they stared at me and did not talk. I then mentioned that the campus had flowers and trees and suchlike, and one student said: "They are ugly; they are all man-made; they did not grow in nature." I asked who had seen a sunset and sunrise, and none of the students had seen one. In China, in many cities big and small, what you see are endless buildings, and children know forests as "forests of buildings." Well-to-do families are able to take their children to travel, but low-income families rarely have the luxury to peek outside of the concrete of the cities.

Amanda: When you grow up in an urban play area, your relationship with nature takes on a different quality. Concrete covers grass and dirt, separating children from the soil, and jungle gyms often have thick foam padding over the dirt to protect children's feet. Skyrises and crowded cityscapes obscure the sunsets and sunrises while ambient light (or pollution) hides the stars at night. As author and journalist Richard Louv points out, "in the city you can't hear anything because you can hear everything," by which he means the overwhelming sounds of the city.[7] For me, living in Beijing, this consisted of the interminable honking of delivery scooters and the pre-recorded welcome messages in convenience stores, which play each time someone enters.

Jing: I was in Hong Kong during the first half of the year in 1997. How I longed to walk on soil! Everywhere I went it was concrete.

People gathered in the horse-racing field, in restaurants, and in stores to spend their relaxation time. This is the life people lived. I lived in a compound and on my first day walking in the garden of the compound I thought I finally could take a walk on some soil; but the earth started to shake—it turns out the shaking was caused by a railroad cart moving underground. I had the same experience in a big open park when I finally thought I could celebrate having soil underneath my feet; then, again, the ground started to shake. It turns out there is a railroad under the park. The city is jacked up by infrastructure and concrete. I visited some friends who lived in an apartment on the 48th floor and felt the distinct lack of oxygen at that height. In urban settings, it is truly a luxury to have soil underneath your feet and to breathe in fresh air as a regular, natural part of the environment.

3. Screens

Today, access to nature isn't always enough to ensure children will venture outside to play. In George Monibot's assessment, it took only one generation in the United Kingdom for "the proportion of children regularly playing in wild places" to fall "from more than half to fewer than 1 in 10," something that is backed up by survey research in the UK funded by the National Trust, which found that children spent only half the time in Nature than their parents did.[8] Similarly, Monbiot says that it took just a six-year period (1997–2003) for the number of children in the United States "with particular outdoor hobbies" to fall by half. As a replacement for outdoor play, or perhaps because opportunities for outdoor play have become more limited, children and teenagers are spending a lot more time on screens: phones, tablets, computers, and televisions.

When I was a child, I was allowed only one hour of television a day. In modern America, the American Academy for Child and Adolescent Psychiatry estimates that children aged eight to twelve "spend 4-6 hours a day watching or using screens, and teens spend up to 9 hours."[9] In Britain, it is estimated that eleven-to-fifteen-year-olds now spend, "on average, half their waking day in front of a screen." These numbers are not, for those of us in education or who have children, surprising. This is not only what children often end up doing, but also what they often beg their parents to *let* them do, a far cry from the days when children begged their parents, as I did, to stay outside with friends, or at the pool. Robin Moore, director of the National Learning Initiative, explains that due to this obsession with screens, for many the primary experience of nature is being replaced by a secondary experience through television and electronic media, which consists of vision and sound only; such an experience strips nature and the world of their more visceral, whole-body meaning.

Today's millennials offer a clear example as more and more of them see computer games and social media as a new kind of modern-day play. Most of the students I teach in Beijing tell me that all they want in the world is thirty more minutes, even ten, or *five*, to play their favorite computer game. On my ten-minute classroom breaks with my students, most of them immediately jump onto social media or start mindlessly watching YouTube videos.

Trying to teach children with a computer in front of them can be extraordinarily challenging; they are pulled into its moving pictures and blinking lights, eager to see how they can manipulate what's in front of them. Even my most diligent and hardworking student, a young girl who carries a copy of Shakespeare's sonnets with her on the weekends, can't stop her fingers from migrating to the keys of my computer when I use it for a dictionary; she is pulled into its possibilities, its endless space all so neatly packaged and contained. If you turn on a television show in a room of children you can count on them dropping everything—chatting, drawing, horseplaying—their mouths relax and their eyes widen as they become absorbed in the story.

Being lost in an animated world seems to have replaced the old, perhaps antiquated idea of "play" in modern, middle-upper class Beijing. This is not surprising when you consider children's busy lives, shuffling endlessly between classes—at school, after school, and on weekends. Schools do provide an hour of recess each day, and a myriad of after-school sports and games, but being on a manicured field, gym, or running track is not the same as being in a forest, in the grass, getting dirt under your fingernails and catching fireflies, especially when half of the year the sky is a cold, poisonous gray.

Students in Beijing are desperate for an escape, and because they did not grow up seeing nature as a refuge, they find it on their screens, much the same way that adults find it in binge-watching a Netflix series. But given how naturally creative we know children can be, it is important for us to ask if they are exercising all the creative muscles they need without outdoor play. What parts of themselves are lost as they languish for hours in front of a screen? What parts of their minds are they *not* developing?

Some argue that for children, technology has become a crutch instead of the tool it was envisioned as being. Frank Wilson, professor of neurology at Stanford, says "these young people are smart, they grew up with computers, they were supposed to be superior—but now we know that something's missing." Although it is astounding how much we can learn in the blink of an eye, some people have come to think the natural world can be experienced through National Geographic, while in reality nothing can replace the visceral experience of being physically present in a place. You can read about the history of China, for example, but can you really form an informed opinion if you haven't been in a Chinese city and seen how people live their lives? Just like reading about meditation and claiming to know what it's like to be transported through mindful breathing, or like "skimming across the surface of the ocean and saying you know all about the sea."

Suggested Reflective Activity #10: The Role of Childhood

We invite you to FREE WRITE on any or all of the following questions:

PART I:

1. Looking back on the microsystem of influences described by Bronfenbrenner, what do you see as the *primary* influences of your childhood?

   o   What stories come to mind?
   o   What stories do you continue to live and tell from your childhood today?

PART II:

2. What role did Nature, specifically, play for you growing up?
3. What messages do you think you were given by your family regarding the importance of "nature" and "play"?
4. If you have children—what are their primary influences, and what do you think are the underlying messages they are being taught due to these?

PART III:

5. What other influences do you think are important to consider other than the three listed here (family, environment, and screens)?

6. If you could design a perfect world for children, what primary influences would you arrange for them to be exposed to regularly? Why?

7. In what ways is your vision *in* or *out* of alignment with your own experience?

   o   How about the experience of people around you?

Scene 7

STORIES FROM TRADITIONAL EDUCATION

*Considering the Hidden Messages of Traditional
Schooling: Three Illuminating Stories from Beijing*

1. Jeselyn

I worked with many students over my time in Beijing whose parents'
goal was to get their children into a top UK or US (private) boarding
school, something they hoped would pave their way to a top UK or
US university. I had one student in particular, whom I will call Jeselyn.
Jeselyn was a thirteen-year-old whose mother enrolled her in a Pre-
SAT course over a one-week vacation in China known as Golden Week.
The course was a grueling one, which required her to arrive at eight
in the morning and leave at ten o'clock at night. While there, she was
expected to memorize upward of one hundred words per day and was
not permitted to leave before proving—through a computer-based
learning system—that she had memorized at least that many.

Before her Pre-SAT course began, Jeselyn and I spent our time
together immersed in fictional stories, which we used to learn about
sentence patterns, writing techniques, and vocabulary. Throughout
class, Jeselyn took the time to color-code her notes in bright pink and
blue ink and always paused our in-class reading to passionately discuss
the characters, seeming emotionally and personally invested in their
stories. After her Pre-SAT course started, however, much of her former
energy and excitement for learning seemed to fade. She explained that
she wasn't getting enough sleep and that her playtime had been reduced
to chatting online with a few friends from the course for thirty minutes
each night, during which they largely commiserated about taking the
Pre-SATs. Her mother warned her ahead of time that if she didn't get
over 1250 on the test she'd have to take it again a few weeks later, a threat
that came to fruition twice in a row before Jeselyn decided to pause our
writing course to focus on her Pre-SATs more fully.

While Jeselyn's achieving a high score on her Pre-SATs will probably
help her get into the school of her choice, the process of studying for and

achieving a high score on a standardized test for school admissions sends her a host of indirect, hidden messages about her worth as a student and the nature of learning. The most prominent of these is that what makes her valuable is not her creativity or critical thinking skills, but her skill at test taking. This can be seen in the fact that this course is intended to be a cram-course, fit into one week's time, with the singular intention of raising her score. The nature of the test itself, which is supposed to be a neutral space for her peers to compete, is made a mockery of by the fact that she can take the test multiple times—this teaches her the added lesson that getting ahead is not about innate ability but about access to resources. She is not really competing with the entire group of test takers, but with those peers who have the same amount of time and money; this group of kids, like Jeselyn, are all willing to sacrifice sleep and playtime to achieve a high score, which teaches her that the world of academia (and professional life in general) is not meant to be enjoyable. Rather, it is hard, grueling work that we put up with to get from point A to point B. Similarly, the prominence of these tests in the admissions process is an indicator of the value these schools place on grades and competition, which effectively sets students up for a life *after* school that values the same things. The entire test-taking industry, not to mention the elite, private school system, seems to abide by an unquestioned functionalist model when it comes to schooling: namely, that school does not exist to create thoughtful, creative, self-actualized people, but, rather, to create a productive, studious workforce who will do their part to keep the workforce moving, with their heads down, generating revenue and feeding into the economy.[1]

Once students get into school, the hidden messages about what is valuable and important only grow stronger and more intense. John Taylor Gatto (quoted in LeFray, 2006) has identified a "hidden curriculum" in traditional schools consisting of "seven invisible lessons," which he argues will shape the way students understand and make sense of the world around them for the rest of their lives.[2] These seven lessons include: confusion, class position, indifference, emotional dependency, intellectual dependency, provisional self-esteem, and the feeling that one can't hide from authority. Four of these that seem particularly impactful to me are confusion, indifference, intellectual dependency, and provisional self-esteem.

Confusion is created for students through the teaching of "disconnected facts with no natural sequence or order," which we see playing out in K-12 history and literature courses focused around "units" without a great deal of investigation into the context of life application. *Indifference* is created by the system of bells ringing between classes, which trains students to refrain from investing in any one topic because of the looming knowledge that they will be cut off when the bell rings, no matter where the teacher is in their lesson—if children are trained to never lose themselves in a particular lesson, to never be swept away by learning, they may conclude that there is no room for passion in the ins and outs of their day. *Intellectual dependency* is created by the classroom structure, which teaches children to look to experts for information and to authority figures for what to do with their day. This teaches students to rely on others rather than to forge their own paths, and ultimately trains them to ignore, let alone trust, their inner wisdom. *Provisional self-esteem* is caused by the testing and grading system, which teaches students that "self-respect depends on the opinions of others" rather than on their own conception of merit. As you can imagine, those students with innate or untamable self-confidence struggle in such a rigid system while those who readily give up their sense of self and happily sacrifice their individuality to the authority of their school are likely to succeed.

Traditional, formal schooling rewards conformity. In such a system, how can we expect students to discover what they are passionate about, or to fall in love with learning? Is it any surprise that some of our most creative minds—Steve Jobs, Bill Gates, Mark Zuckerberg, and Oprah Winfrey, to name a few—drop out of school before it is complete? Or that learning has come to be seen as a chore to get through rather than an indulgence of the intellectual and sensual capacities?

Why is learning not considered, instead, to be a personal, or even spiritual opportunity? What kinds of creative genius are we stifling by forcing students to conform to arbitrary rules and suppress their holistic, critical, independent thinking? Why not use school as a place to encourage children to fall in love with learning? To discover their powerful, unique voice? Why not allow them space and time in school to develop their dreams?

2. Ariel

While working in Beijing I had the pleasure of teaching a number of truly gifted students one-on-one, giving me a front row seat to the kinds of talents and passions children carry. One who stands out was a twelve-year-old girl who came to me because she needed to improve her English before applying to schools in the United Kingdom (let's call her Ariel). I didn't need more than a few minutes with Ariel to clearly see her passion: creative writing.

At twelve years old, she had already written a novel in Chinese. Her mother, determined that Ariel should learn English and move to the UK, demanded she stop writing in Chinese. But Ariel was determined, and so in order to continue writing her novel she started working on it in school where her mother was unable to monitor her. Finding time amid a heavily scripted schedule proved challenging, but Ariel accomplished it by sneaking her laptop into the girl's toilet during lunch and free periods, huddling in the corner of an out-of-the-way bathroom on the second floor for privacy. This led to a series of unlikely friendships with a small group of similarly frustrated girls who retreated to the bathroom to do makeup or gossip. After I had worked with Ariel for over a year, she finally finished her novel and secretly published it on the web where people could buy access for 50 yuan (about $7.50). She quickly sold nearly five hundred copies!

Clearly Ariel, at twelve years old, already has an innate, deeply felt passion. However, her environment—parents, teachers, and the system of elite private school education—do not see the usefulness of her passion in a world where English-speaking and STEM fields are thought to be her best chance at a comfortable life. If Ariel wants to retain her passion, she will need to find ways to work on it *despite* her surroundings. What if her schedule—which currently consists of school Monday through Friday, piano all day Saturday, and math and English class on Sunday—were formatted around her personality? What if she were given free time to use as she liked—to work on her novel, or just to go outside and explore, or even to play? What parts of her creative, artistic mind would evolve if she was able to explore nature on the weekends? How would her stories change?

Jing: When I was doing research in China from 2000 to 2012, I often got referred to by colleagues as an expert to give parents advice on their children's decision to enroll in a certain university. Many parents simply decided for their children what major to enroll in or what university to attend. Once a student was admitted into a university of his dreams, but his parents wanted him to attend another one with a higher reputation but which had no major that met his passion. On many occasions, when I polled students during my talks in colleges about how many of them had their parents decide for them to study their major, majority of the students raised their hands. Some students were in tears when they shared that they really did not like their field of study and that they felt stuck and hopeless. An American colleague of mine carried out a study which showed that more than 80 percent of American students made their college choice on their own, or together with a counselor or their parents, while more than 80 percent of Chinese students had their parents make the decision for them, sometimes with their class director (a teacher in charge of students' daily study and discipline). We shared the research finding with the Chinese audience and they all nodded their heads confirming the finding.

3. Luna

One night in Beijing, around seven o'clock, I was finishing up a poetry class with a student. She took a break from the writing she was doing, looked up, and said, "I think a lot about where we come from and why we exist, and some people say it's God, but I think the Earth is God, because without the Earth, we won't exist, and without the Universe, the Earth won't exist."

I smiled at her, put down my pen, and sat back in my chair to give her my full attention. "Do you think we are connected to the trees and the animals?" I asked.

"Yes," she answered quickly. "We are animals, we're just the smartest ones."

I wanted to hug her and cry; she understood the interconnection of all living things innately, at just seven years old, while many spend their whole lives unable to grasp this connection. She understood it despite growing up in an urban metropolis where the sky is covered in gray half the time, the sun and stars regularly unseen beneath the thick smog that covers the city. Her reflection came simply and directly, unprompted, from the heart of her being. This type of thinking needs to be recognized and encouraged by parents and teachers when it occurs naturally, but first, it needs to be allowed to develop—in our current schooling model, it must be asked: Are we giving students this opportunity?

If education is to be a tool for achieving peace and balance in the world, where we take only what we need and balance is retained in the delicate ecosystem, then we will need to build an educational system that creates opportunities for students to feel love and respect for all living beings. Taoists understand this concept well, emphasizing that the world was not made for humans alone, and that its natural state is one of deep interconnectedness between all living things.[3] In this conception, the balance we need cannot be achieved by grabbing, possessing, or accumulating, yet these are the values stressed by our capitalist, for-profit system.

If our leaders were educated to value their connection with nature over material possession as children, perhaps they would channel their enormous energy, with all its fire and determination to make things happen, into pursuits that deepened our communion with nature rather than our dominance over it . . . if this was the message given to children through their schooling, and backed up by a society that valued and rewarded these things, the world would be a very different place, indeed.

A Story of Environmental Education (EE) in China: Lessons About Teaching EE

In 1978 a proposal was formally made in China to integrate Environmental Protection (EP) into the curriculum for Chinese elementary and secondary schools. By 1979 it was being incorporated into science, geography, and chemistry textbooks followed by training workshops in how to teach EP for teachers. Soon sustainable development (SD) had become a "top priority in China's development and reform agenda," leading to the implementation of a nationwide EE program in 1996.[4]

While the implementation of the EE curriculum shows awareness of and commitment to positive change in China, a survey conducted at two elementary schools and two secondary schools in Nanning in 2018 made it clear that the implementation was poorly executed. From 216 respondents who filled out questionnaires, Chengqiang et al. discovered that the way the national program had been instituted and carried out did not do justice to the topic, stopping well short of transformation. Results showed that although the majority of students (76.7%) agreed that "environmental protection is very important and the environment must be protected by everyone right now," these same individuals admitted that "they would throw away used paper, bottles, or empty lunch boxes in a public place if they could not find a trash can and while nobody was watching." The difference between these students' thoughts and actions illuminates the powerful difference between learning a fact, *understanding* it, and acting on it. If the students enrolled in the EE curriculum had truly come to understand the life cycle of a product, and if they truly *felt* their connection to the earth or their responsibility for the future, they might not have been so cavalier about littering.

Chengqiang et al.'s report uncovered one possible culprit for the lack of student care for littering and the environment, which was that while teachers did present "environmental knowledge in their teachings," as was required, they did not go beyond the material provided by the government. They did not take field trips or do hands-on activities to make the subject stand out for students, and they did not "self- study EE materials or discuss EE issues with other subject teachers." This begs the question: What if students had been taken out into nature to feel the power of the environment? What if they had visited an especially dirty area of their city or town and spent an afternoon cleaning up other people's litter? What if they had been asked to deeply reflect on what keeps them alive on this planet, or what is bound to happen if their generation does not begin to place value on this life-giving system?

The breakdown between policy and implementation in China underscores the importance of creative teaching methods, not to mention teacher training and support. It underscores the importance of teachers feeling passionately about their subject, especially when it comes to the environment—if teachers don't feel passionately about their subject, it will be hard for them to impart any sort of deep passion to their students. If schools hope to revolutionize students' relationship to the environment, then students will need a lot more than an introduction to facts and statistics. They will need a deeply felt relationship to the Earth so that they don't just *learn about* the facts but connect with nature spiritually, and open themselves to feel her love, and even *hear her cries* for protection. They need an integration of *yin* and *yang* in their learning, where cognitive learning happens along with the cultivation of compassion, love, and protective instincts, so that a new way of seeing the earth will take root in their heart and spirit as well as their mind. We believe that it is only with this integrated, whole-body learning that there is any chance of such a connection continuing *after* the class is over.

Suggested Reflective Activity #11: Considering Your Experience with Education

We invite you to FREE WRITE on any or all of the following questions:

1. Whether obvious/overt or subtle/understated, how would you describe your family's approach to, or message about, learning?

2. What other messages did you receive from your extended family, or larger community, about education and learning?

   ○ How did this affect you throughout your life . . . how did it come to define (or not) your educational journey?

3. In your school experience, what messages do you think you were being sent about what was valuable?

   – What messages were sent by the grading system?
   – What messages were sent by the structure of the school?
   – What messages, if any, were sent about the role of Nature?
   – What messages were sent about the importance of play?

4. Thinking back over your school experience, what do you think could be changed for future generations, without sacrificing education, which would help ensure we are teaching children to respect and love the environment?

Scene 8

EDUCATION AS A PLAYGROUND FOR CHANGE
THREE INSPIRATIONAL STORIES

1. Contemplative Education: Attending to the Nonthinking Brain as Education Pedagogy

Contemplative Education refers to the movement among educators and scholars to integrate the lessons that arise through an active contemplative practice into education pedagogy. The lessons of contemplative practice are centered around an awareness of the interconnection of all living beings, and the cultivation of essential values that the world is sorely missing, like compassion, love, and gratitude, which arise naturally when you open yourself to the energy of the universe. This energy is described by Sun and Lin as an energy that "cannot be named, predicted, or described," yet which, when properly cultivated, causes "the human being's mind, body, and spirit to function in synergy with the energy, spirit, matter, and information of the universe," so that the universe flows both with and through us.[1] Tapping into this energy through meditation brings the practitioners a sense of peace and love, which radiates through their bodies and out into their lives. Physicist and author Arthur Zajonc writes that the goal of contemplative work is to join "insight and compassion" as well as "wisdom and love" in the mind, body, and soul of the practitioner.[2] Contemplative education, therefore, is predicated upon the contemplative practice of the teacher— if peace, love, and gratitude are cultivated in the practitioner, they will slip out into the world through the practitioner's thoughts, actions, and relationships.

Contemplative educators use their personal practice to cultivate love and compassion toward their students and believe in an approach to education that honors the whole being (heart, mind, *and* spirit). Its practitioners argue that integrating contemplative practice into education has the power to transform education from a hierarchical, knowledge-passing system (from teacher *to* student) into a values-based practice of knowledge-sharing (between and *among* the teacher, her students, and the entire living ecosystem) that not only integrates all parts of our being (mind, body, spirit) but also works to cultivate a worldview that loves and honors all living beings.[3] Moreover, in a course developed by an engaged contemplative practitioner, academic knowledge is taught alongside moral and spiritual wisdom, which is essential for cultural transformation, not to mention the fostering of world peace and ecological stewardship.[4]

Practices explored by contemplative educators include, but are not limited to, breath and movement-based practices, such as meditation, yoga, tai chi, and qigong as well as arts or writing-based practices, such as storytelling, painting, and reflective writing, among others. These practices help teachers and students create a more creative, engaged, interdependent classroom community that values all kinds of learning and knowing (spiritual, corporeal, experiential, intuitive, logical, etc.) and creates a classroom ethic that sees students as unique, worthy, and knowledgeable. By engaging in these practices, contemplative educators commit to dismantling false hierarchies of power in the classroom and cultivating classrooms that honor the interdependence of all living beings.

I (Amanda) was introduced to contemplative education by my coauthor (Jing) in 2016, through a course she still teaches today at the University of Maryland entitled *Contemplative Inquiry & Holistic Education*. Although I had been a passionate and engaged teacher for most of my career, a few years before Jing's course I had accepted a Lecturer position in Academic Writing. The Academic Writing program was enormous, and their basic course was required for all students in the university, which meant that a large pool of graduate students were giving teaching assistantships that included teaching this class. These teachers were often young and inexperienced, having never taught a class before in their lives, and so to support these teachers the program created a standardized curriculum, which included standardized assignments, readings, and writing assignments. Use of the standardized curriculum was required only for the first semester, after which experienced teachers were welcome to become creative with the assignments and the syllabus. Despite this invitation to be creative, however, I had used the standardized syllabus as an excuse to stop investing time in developing relationships with my students— rather than engaging with my heart and whole being, as I had done prior to taking up the job of lecturer, I was showing up each day and teaching the material in someone else's voice, with someone else's classroom activities and materials. Later, through meditation, I realized that I had been engaged in what contemplative practitioners call "an objectification of my own teaching experience," cynically going through the motions of teaching in a way that objectified the act itself, as well as my students.[5]

One of the assignments in Jing's course was for each student to take on a daily meditative practice of some kind. This could be traditional sitting meditations, or more active daily activities, like meditative eating, reflective writing, drawing, yoga, or tai chi. Meditative practitioners, religious leaders, and contemplative theorists alike have described the goal of meditation as learning to recognize and let go of our distracting engagement with thoughts, responsibilities, and ego, opening ourselves to the expansive universe of energy and love that is always around us. Arthur Zajonc describes it as a way to move beyond the thinking mind and connect with our "silent self," which "acts from a place beyond ego."[6] John Miller describes it as leaving behind our "fragmented consciousness," where we are "pushed and pulled by the outside world," and discovering a deeply attentive and engaged state of contemplative awareness.[7]

> **Jing**: In ancient times in China, when an artist prepared to draw or to write calligraphy, the creative process was considered to be sacred, and the artist would enter a meditative state, refraining from anger and sex, eating a vegetarian diet, meditating for days before working on the artwork. It is believed in this state of full integration of one's body, heart, mind, and spirit, one can tap into the creative energy of Dao, gaining the support of spirits and imprinting or projecting vivid, life energy qi onto the artwork so that it comes out as an artwork with a life of its own. Doing art is like creating life; it is a sacred act. The best artworks are, then, considered those that have spirit and energy.[8]

For Jing's class, I decided to commit myself to daily meditation. Over the weeks that followed, I found the meditative practice I took to be unexpectedly, but *fully*, transformative. I reflected on the impact of the meditation in reflective journals, a portion of which has been excerpted here:

> Upon closing my eyes, and turning my attention outward, I was overwhelmed by what came rushing in around me: an energy so alive with love, wholeness, and strength that it filled the entirety of my

being. I felt called to go outside, and so in the park near my house, on a warm summer afternoon, I clasped my hands behind my back and started walking.

People were everywhere: some in groups, enjoying picnics in one another's company, others riding bikes or playing games. I will never forget the way I felt as I passed one particular group of friends sitting on a blanket they had spread beneath a tree; they seemed in love with their shared space, talking, passing food, laughing happily. In my meditative state, I was able to *feel* something uniquely and perfectly human: I felt that we shared the same past, the same future, the same joy, and the same intense suffering. I felt that there was more that connected us than separated us, and because of this, I had intense love for them, as well as joyful empathy.[9]

I quickly realized that I had been treating my students as less than the unique, worthy human souls that they were, and that to revitalize my classes I needed to find ways to engage them personally in the learning. I needed to show them that I respected their individual stories and knowledge.

Because I am a writer, I chose to engage my students in a storytelling activity that dovetailed with the work of academic writing, and so I created an assignment called the "Daily Brief." As part of the Daily Brief, at least one of my students would start the class each day by telling a story from their personal experience, followed by thoughtful questions for the class that engaged with what we were learning that week about rhetoric and writing. As soon as I designed and implemented the activity, my classroom was transformed from a place of lethargy, disinterest, and disrespect to a room full of students who were fully awake, engaged, and eager to go on whatever educational journey I had in mind. They trusted me! This was a natural human response to the daily practice of sharing and discussing one another's personal stories.

Although it was not a requirement for my students to share anything personal, many chose to share stories that were surprisingly difficult— they were stories of death, inner conflict, and deep anxiety, which I was honored to be trusted with. Their classmates jumped at the chance to support one another, volunteering similar experiences or sharing deep empathy. It soon became clear that they were using the assignment to not only build community with one another, but to also learn and grow through writing, which was an essential skill for my course.

Through engaging with my students as unique human souls and giving them the opportunity to engage with the course personally, I fell back in love with teaching. I learned that education that does not allow for spiritual and emotional knowledge in addition to intellectual knowledge misses the opportunity to make education meaningful for students. When classroom conversation moves beyond the academic to the personal, a classroom community is formed—when the classroom becomes a community, learning takes on a personal quality, which can leave a much deeper mark on students' beings. In the process, we transform the classroom from a teacher centered, one-way knowledge-passing space to an interconnected learning environment where transformative learning is possible.

My story is just one example of the power of contemplative practice in the classroom. It starts with the teacher's own practice and cannot develop without it. From the teacher's personal practice comes the cultivation of deep love, respect, and kindness in her heart, which will have a natural ripple effect into her classroom. Through her orientation toward contemplative values, she will transform the way lessons are designed and help orient her students around these same values.[10] In this way, contemplative practice has the power to transform education into a powerful, love-centered experience that engages the whole being: mind, body, and spirit.

Connecting Contemplative Education and Social Justice

Contemplative educators want much more for their classrooms than improved classroom community and more engaged lessons. The practice of meditation is one way to experience the interconnection and interdependence of all living things, which our consumer culture has been slowly undoing. Both contemplative practitioners and environmental educators argue that if we want to lay a strong foundation for sustainable living, we need to first rediscover this link between ourselves and all other living beings. If education is to be a tool for cultivating a new transformative vision—from an isolated self to an interconnected one—then considering ways to centralize contemplative practice in education is one way to do it. Contemplative educators argue that through developing this link in our students between their whole beings and the rest of the world (humans and nonhumans), we will be helping to form students who are ready to create the change we need. As Sun and Lin entreat their readers, "we must bring 'soul' back to education" and teach students more than "book knowledge," showing them the satisfaction and inner peace that is available when they choose to "seek inner richness rather than outer wealth."[11] If we accept that belief in an interconnected state of all living things has the power to transform our global value system from one of consumerism and greed to one of sustainability and peace, then educators who give their students the opportunity to experience this state bring us one step closer to transformative change with each class they teach.

2. Democratic Schooling

One of my closest and oldest of friends, Louise, lives amid the Pyrenees in the south of France with her husband and two children. I visited her in the summer of 2017, and was immediately convinced that she was giving her children an enormous gift by having them grow up in such a place. When her children walk outside each morning, it's into a garden that overlooks rolling hills and mountains flanked in every direction by wide open green space. Her children play outside every day, in the fresh mountain air, among trees and plants and animals. They need to go out of their way to find a shopping mall, a Starbucks, or even a bit of traffic.

When Louise's children started school in the village, the teachers complained that her eldest son had trouble sitting still and doing his work. They suggested he might have a learning problem, but Louise knew that this was not the case; he was the sort of boy who read history books for entertainment and was able to engage for long hours when his interest was piqued. The problem was simple: he was a young boy who needed to get up and move around more frequently in order to then sit still for long periods. He was also, for better or worse, a boy who knew what he was interested in and what he was not—he wouldn't be cajoled into learning something he found boring or unimportant. Louise didn't want to demand that her son lose these qualities in order to fit into a predetermined style of learning; she felt sure there were other possibilities.

Fortunately, Louise met a woman in her village who was looking into alternatives for traditional schooling and invited her to join their planning group, which was actively discussing opening a democratic school in the village. They were researching the school in earnest when I visited in 2017. In an article Louise sent me on democratic schooling by psychologist and Boston College professor Peter Gray, it is asserted on the first page that "education, broadly defined, is cultural transmission."[12] I paused over that line; in effect, the idea of school as cultural transmission has its roots in functionalism, positioning education as functionally responsible for imbuing children with their first ideas about the structure and value of our cultural imaginary. But rather than taking a traditional approach, which imagines students' role in society as good workers, democratic schools imagine their students as change-makers and leaders who believe in the power of their own voice.

In his article, Gray argues that our current cultural understanding of education is flawed due to its focus on forced learning—tests, required number of classes, emphasis on grades, and rule-following. Such an approach will produce followers, not leaders, while stifling any chance at transformative learning or creative thinking for its students. Proponents of Democratic Schooling critique traditional schooling for its orientation toward producing productive citizens who accumulate wealth and grow the economy (to serve the state), implying that such a goal for our children is deficient and selfish—it is a *societal* goal, not an individualized life goal, and therefore not good enough for children. A contemplative educator might add that such a goal does not honor the unique human soul in each child, therefore stifling the learner and the learning process.

A primary goal of democratic schooling is to "unschool" children by removing them from the dominant worldview produced by the "industrial education system," which in effect teaches children to be good workers and value external gratification.[13] Instead, democratic schools encourage students to develop their own paradigm of knowledge and learning acquisition, similar to contemplative educators who argue that "subjectivity" and "direct personal experiences" are powerful ways of learning and knowing, which should be embraced.[14] In essence, children in a democratic schooling environment are given the absolute freedom to direct their learning however they like. The purpose is *not* to learn specific subjects, or even specific skills, but to explore and understand their individual character while participating in an engaged learning community. For the school Louise and her friends opened in the Ariege, which they call the Pleine Nature School, this means helping students to develop goals for their learning that are extensions of their personal interests. If their interest is to play, the adult facilitators on the staff will help the students to find a goal aligned with that interest, such as building a tree house or leading a field trip. Louise's eldest son currently has the goal of learning Russian, and so has taken on the responsibility of funding Russian teachers. To reach this goal he had to make a proposal to hire a Russian teacher, which included a commitment to sell hot chocolate and contribute his earnings to their salaries. Whatever goal students decide on, the important piece is that they take responsibility—mapping out each required step and doing the majority of the work themselves, with minimal supervision, on a reasonable timeline.

The learning community and its decision-making apparatus is perhaps the most important and impressive feature of a democratic school. At the Pleine Nature School, decisions are made by the school as a community, where the voice of the children is equal to that of the adult facilitators. Louise tells me that, in fact, the adults try to stay out of the meetings because their tendency is to dominate the conversation; they prefer to let the students take control themselves, making mistakes, recognizing those mistakes, and learning from them as a community. In keeping with this philosophy, every rule in the school is proposed and voted on by the students, and when a rule is broken or someone at the school is offended or upset by another student, there is a student-led process (based on the principles of sociocracy) to decide on the consequences for the concerned party or parties.[15]

In addition to decision-making authority, the children at Pleine Nature School decide on their own learning priorities. In keeping with French law, the school provides access to all the same subjects required by the public school curriculum, but the students decide on their own which classes they will take. If there is a class or hobby they want to learn that is not offered, they will make a proposal to create a student club or hire a teacher. When a child makes a proposal, it is taken to the weekly school meeting for discussion and debate—first the student will introduce the proposal with reasons, then answer any questions from the other students to tease out the details, followed by a vote. If anyone has an objection, their objection will be voiced, and the student will have a chance to reformulate his/her proposal, negotiating it again and again until all students agree.

Through the school's student-led decision-making bodies, the students learn how organizations are run, how decisions are made, and the impact of taking a position and making an argument when people are really listening. The students then get to witness the decisions they make being enacted, and so they experience their decisions as real-world decisions with consequences for their learning environment and the larger learning community. This teaches them to think about the structures in which they live and learn, and to consider what can and should change.

Each morning the schedule for the day is posted and students decide on what they will do for the day. If they prefer to stay outside and play all day, no one will stop them—that is their choice. The children will not be forced to do anything aside from treating themselves, the school, and one another with respect, showing up each day as engaged members of the learning community. As perhaps is obvious, the goal of Pleine Nature School is to allow students to come to learning on their own, believing that if they refrain from imposing learning on the students as is done in traditional schools, the students will, through a structure devoid of pressure and conformity, fall in love with learning on their own time, in their own way. Aside from attending the required meeting, participating in Justice Circles, and creating projects that help them achieve their learning goals, the students are free to decide on their own what to do with their time. Some of them might choose to play every day for six months, engaging only in play-related projects, but Louise tells me that eventually the students come to yearn for a classroom environment. This is the magical moment for democratic educators: that moment when a child finds a passion for learning of his/her own free will. This, they believe, will be a learning that will stay with them for the rest of their lives.

In a model where children choose what to do with their time, of course, it should be no surprise that they spend an enormous amount of time playing outdoors, which Louise and her friends see as enormously valuable. She describes their games as complex and intelligently designed, often going on for months at a time. The children form teams and an intricate system of rules and boundaries that can keep them engaged from the moment they arrive at the school until the moment they are picked up by their parents without anyone telling them to stop. For Louise, this *is* learning; she cites skills like mutual cooperation, group work, leadership, rulemaking/breaking, and creativity; it goes without saying that a teacher at almost any other school would quickly label this as "off-task behavior" and require the children to stop. At the Pleine Nature School adults do not have the authority to discipline children on the spot—just like the students, when they see someone breaking a rule they will need to put in a request for a Justice Circle hearing and follow the process. And if the adults do something that upsets the children, they also must face their own Justice Circles to reestablish peace and balance.

Evidence of the students' creativity can be seen in the clubs they have created. Some of the nature-oriented ones include a tree club, a nature club, a farm machinery club, a cooking club, and an ecological school club with film and debate. They also have clubs for comic book making, creative writing, Manga, graffiti, stop-motion anime, and vlogging (among others too numerous to name).

Whether Louise's students are leaning "enough" is up to the reader to judge, but what is clear is that this model of education undoes the "hidden curriculum," allowing students to develop a certain strength of mind and character that will no doubt serve them well in the future. While some may worry that they have trouble adapting to a nine-to-five work week, children with this kind of freedom at school will likely have the kind of out-of-the-box thinking needed to transform a business or reimagine programming. The school's focus on child-led learning also answers calls by some scholars for education that is more intuitive and wisdom-based in that students can follow their passions, whatever those may be. While it is not the only possible way to transform our current system, it does represent a clear shift from our dominant worldview as Westerners, and our traditional approach to thinking. As Louv reminds us, the traditional model is unlikely to help us solve problems like climate change, which require the boldness and determination to believe in the possibility of transformative change.[16] It seems sensible, after all, that if what we need is cultural and societal transformation, these solutions are unlikely to be found using the traditional educational models, which were present when the problem was created.

Jing: When my older daughter was little, one day I was boiling a lobster, and seeing the lobster turning red in the boiling water, she asked me: "Mommy, does the lobster hurt?" I was a bit shocked because I had taught myself to be numb to the suffering of other species and treat them as delicious food. She, in her "innocence," however, sensed the pain of the lobster. For a long time, she often painted a group of little pigs with one cute little pig having one eye half-closed. I did not get it until one day I asked her, and she pointed to the toy set of little porgies that I had bought for her and one of them has one eye half-closed. Children are observing. They connect with nature intuitively and spiritually. One poem she wrote when she was in middle school talked about how she picks an autumn leaf to preserve that has defects from among the thousands of beautiful leaves, for no one would love this one while others received praises. She wanted to give love to the leaf that no one would love. Maria Montessori says that children are highly intelligent and spiritual, and they are teachers of adults. If we design curriculum and schools according to the spiritual quality of the children, affirm their precious traits, and learn humbly from them, what kind of world will we have?

My younger daughter did not show too strong a tendency for nature until she was in college. One day she saw a video of cute little pigs being fried alive, and she was so devastated that she cried for days, and she has since become a vegan. Not only that, but she has also been promoting vegan food, becoming an expert in making vegan cookies and cakes and selling them to a sizable clientele, and her creativity is fully manifested as she treats them as works of art and with love. The reviews and feedback she has got from clients and friends support her passion and give her a lot of aspirations.

3. Universities

One week while in Beijing, I was invited to attend a lecture from a professor of engineering and computer science at Stanford University. He was pitching Stanford to a small group of Chinese parents and the primary point he chose to focus on was how much money their children could make if they went to Stanford. He started off with Stanford's world ranking, then proudly explained that the average salary for graduates of his program was $100,000 per year. He reminded us multiple times that one of his own classmates had started Google and hinted at their own children's potential future success in one of Silicon Valley's big-name companies, who he assured them would be recruiting at Stanford due to its close proximity. Despite my distaste for his value system (wealth- and prestige-focused), I paid careful attention—*breathe this in,* I told myself, *this is the state of things, and you need to understand it.*

If I had only ever been in rooms like that one, with the great majority of attendees tacitly agreeing that the accumulation of wealth is a valid goal in life, and that education is a means to some disembodied financial end rather than our best hope for transforming the world through growth and discovery, then I may not have ever been exposed to the sorts of beliefs in these pages. I may not have had any idea about the movement, among forward-thinking institutions, to transform education into something that will not just produce graduates capable of performing well at companies but that will also work toward the betterment of *all* people and *all* life on this planet.

My own university experience was one of self-growth and discovery. My professors did not try to mold me into a productive member of a capitalist society; in fact, they did not even *discuss* my future career with me. My university, and many like it, were committed to educating its graduates as whole people and engaged citizens, prioritizing the creation of a liminal space where young minds could feel free to evolve and change, blooming with wondrous colors in the wilderness of intellectual possibility. It focused on self-enrichment, curiosity, and exposure to ideas that would open hearts and minds.

My university experience was filled with performances of poetry and music, which have stayed with me to this day; inspiring lectures on religion, philosophy, and art; long walks in nature; and classes whose intellectual coursework spilled out into my regular life. Its goal did not seem to be, from my perspective, to prepare me for the cutthroat world of competition and accumulation that they knew would await. In fact, it may even have been the express lack of these conversations that kept me idealistic enough to follow my dreams—first to Asia, where I stayed for six years, then Greenpeace, then a Master's in creative writing. It did not prepare me to make a high salary or buy fancy things, but to know myself well, and consider the world as a conundrum of intellectual and spiritual questions I wanted to spend my life exploring. I did not leave university with a five-year plan, but with a full heart and an open mind.

We (Amanda and Jing) believe that universities can, and should be, one of the places we look to when considering how we will engage the next generation in the kind of transformative societal change we need. Before we continue, we'd like to pause for a moment and share our stories.

Amanda's University Story

In high school I was a B student. This wasn't because I couldn't get A's, but because by and large, I found my high school education uninteresting. It wasn't until I attended my first college class at St. Mary's College of Maryland, where I did my Bachelor's degree, that I realized education could be any other way. One of the first classes I took was the history of apartheid with an energetic teacher named Gerrey Deenie, who had once written speeches for Nelson Mandela, something he told us on the first day. Professor Dennie made the course come alive through his impassioned speeches and personal examples. He assigned us Nelson Mandela's *Long Walk to Freedom,* and for the first time in my life I found myself voluntarily staying up all night to finish an assigned reading. In high school I hated history, but at St. Mary's I found myself unable to stop taking history classes! The history of Russia and China were next, and with each course came books of literature and philosophy that I had never before associated with history, along with teachers whose personal interest in the subject was contagious. To my delight, learning was transformed before me into an engaging, beautiful thing!

We did not take tests but read and wrote essays. I found myself personally devoted to my writing, to the extent that my hands shook as I turned in my essays, eager to hear what my professors would say. And history was not the only subject that astounded me: my literature, philosophy, writing, and art courses were equally intriguing. I became so impassioned by class after class that I had trouble deciding what to major in, eventually switching from English to history, then history to philosophy, and finally compromising by taking twenty-four credits a semester (16 were required) so that I could spend my "free time" learning to write poems, draw, and paint. This was a completely new kind of learning—learning that engaged my heart as well as my mind.

In addition to the courses, St. Mary's geography offered an introduction to the power of the natural world which deepened learning. Its campus sits on a wide bend in the St. Mary's River where the land juts out in a curved peninsula, giving the appearance of water on two sides. It is built on the historic site of St. Mary's City, founded in 1634, which means that parts of the campus are literally steeped in and surrounded by history. This is especially poignant in some of the older buildings, like the honors dormitory where I spent my freshman and sophomore years. It was a two-story manor house with a sweeping front porch and rooms of varying shapes and sizes, which used to function as a nuns' seminary. Its front yard includes a tiny graveyard dating back to the 1600s and a one-room church with stunning stained glass windows. A short walk down the hill from the church you will find a path leading to the sandy banks of St. Mary's River. The land of the beach juts out into a kind of tip, which students at St. Mary's call "the point"; on it a large wooden cross is planted, like a marker of a forgotten time.

Students are lucky to be so close to the beach. They can come whenever they like to sink their bare feet into the beach lined with pebbles and beautiful old trees. It is a place where I sat many afternoons and evenings watching the sunset, writing in my journal, overwhelmed by the natural beauty. Proximity to these things meant finding refuge in quiet green spaces for reading, writing, or wrestling with ideas, which helped me to experience the power of nature to extend and deepen learning. I did not just learn the content of my classes, or the material essay assignments, but a sense of learning *quality* extended by the physical environment, which I now understand can encourage intellectual engagement. As I walked along the banks of St. Mary's River, wandered through ancient headstones, or spent the evening debating with my impassioned peers, I was forming an understanding of higher education's role as one that is both honorable and transformative.

Back in 2000, when I graduated, the college had less than 1,600 students. This meant that even our lower-level, required courses were able to run with thirty students or less, while our upper-level courses could be as small as eight students. As a philosophy major, my upper-level courses were discussion-based and often held in intimate spaces: the houses of professors, upperclassmens' townhomes, or intimate rooms with whitewashed walls and round wooden tables. It was rare if a professor lectured, and if a lecture was given, it was always inspirational as well as informative. Much more common were discussion-based courses whose tone and tenor felt like heated dinner conversations between friends and family. Perhaps because of this, I developed personal relationships with my professors, some of whom I am still in touch with today. Many encouraged us to see them as equals, not only inviting us into their homes, but also engaging with us in debate, going out of their way to take our young minds seriously. The time I spent with my professors—sitting in their offices long after the class had ended, sending emails back and forth long after I had left the St. Mary's campus—are by far the things I cherish most about my college experience. These were made possible by the structure and philosophy of the school: its small student population, commitment to a liberal arts curriculum, and emphasis on engaged, meaningful learning.

Since St. Mary's I have attended two other universities: San Diego State University for my Master's degree, and the University of Maryland at College Park for my doctorate. While neither of these universities have the kind of green space offered by St. Mary's, or the same amount of intimately small classes, they faithfully embodied the kind of intellectual engagement and openness of ideas we associate with universities. This is, after all, *the role* of the university: to challenge students' beliefs, expose them to new ideas, and teach them to be critical and creative thinkers in the hope that they will deepen and expand their capacity for knowing. If this is done well, they will then apply that thoughtfully for the rest of their lives.

The Challenge of Transformative Change
At St. Mary's, I once ran from a poetry class in tears after my professor—once poet-laureate of Maryland, Lucille Clifton—told me, in a careful voice, that the poem I had turned in for a workshop

wasn't working. "You're hiding behind your words," she said. "You're not letting the reader in on the thing you really want to say." Despite the close relationship I had cultivated with her through late-night conversations in her office, and despite the deep respect I had for her life, career, and poems, in that moment I resented her in a desperate, angry way.

It was a night class, and so when class let out it was already dark outside. Grateful for the cover of night, I ran to the middle of the grass quad, sat by myself, and cried. The whole time I cried I called her names in my mind, swearing that I would never return to that class, or read another one of her poems. Then, once my tears had dried, I took up my pen and wrote my first honest poem. The next week I submitted that poem proudly to our workshop and beamed as Lucille praised what I had done.

Today, when I look back at that moment, I am grateful to Lucille Clifton for her honesty; I know that if I had not experienced the difficulty of shame and embarrassment that accompanied being told the truth in front of my classmates, I would never have made that important shift in my writing.

Transformative change is never pleasant, especially when we are young and full of insecurities. I was lucky to experience this more than once at St. Mary's; the second time it happened as the result of an independent study I created with my favorite philosophy professor, John Schroeder, on Buddhism. I wanted to become an expert in Buddhism, and felt sure the learning would be easy, but, instead, the first concept Professor Schroeder gave me was "nonself." For me, at the time, the idea of "nonself" felt like the annihilation of individuality and all that came with it, which I was sure was a terrible thing. No matter how I tried to explain my thoughts on the concept to Professor Schroeder, sure I was right, the result was always the same: he would shake his head apologetically, telling me I just didn't understand it and needed to continue thinking.

At first, these conversations were frustrating; Professor Schroeder answered everything I said with what sounded to me like a riddle, insisting that my negative take on the concept was simply not right. But no matter how hard I tried, the idea of believing in such a thing kept on feeling like a mistake—why would I want to give up who I am? Or to deny my personal passions and intense feelings? I was attached to those things!

I remember one afternoon, as I recounted all the reasons I did not want to give up my deep, impassioned emotions—why I thought those things were an essential part of life—Professor Schroeder smiled and told me that "nonattachment is not the same thing as detachment."

What! I wanted to scream.

I began to feel as if I was too stupid or brainwashed to ever understand and quickly began to feel overwhelmed by the question, approaching a state of intellectual frenzy and irritation I had never quite experienced. But I trusted Professor Schroeder completely, and so rather than pushing the discomfort away, I threw myself into it, determined to find my way.

I went to his office every free moment I could, laying my questions at his feet, braving his sly smile at my passionate desperation. He suggested a few other students for me to reach out to, and I did this dutifully. I felt comfortable enough to *share* my discomfort and *reveal* my struggle even though it was embarrassing. Rather than slinking behind my fear, I wrote, thought, and talked about the concept of nonself relentlessly, with anyone who would listen or brave the conversation with me.

It took several weeks, but finally, at long last, it clicked: I realized that nonself is about freedom, not annihilation. It doesn't ask us to deny who we are, but to let go of our ego-identity. To stop clinging to what we think we know about who we are—the ideology we have constructed about the "self"—and to, instead, find a peaceful state of nonattachment from ego (and self) so that we can see the world with fully opened eyes. We do not cease to be who we are, but, rather, let go of the constructs we have created.

> **Jing:** Nonself is also the other side of the Self. We think we are individual beings but, instead, we are every bit dependent on others and on nature: we don't produce most of the food we consume; the clothes we wear; we did not pave the road we travel on; we literally rely on others to live, hence everyone is us. The Buddhist idea of no-self goes into the deeper realm of reality, that is, we are energies in the vast spectrums of vibration of the universe, and there is no self but someone in relation to others and others in relation to us. We inter-are. We inter-exist. When we realize this a tremendous sense of gratitude arises for the blessings and grace we are bestowed by the selfless giving of countless others to make our being, as a self, possible. So the nonself is also many selfs' self. Inter-being it is.

The idea of nonself was one of the most difficult things I have ever had to learn. Why? Because it was a completely new way of conceiving of the world, and at twenty years old, it was the first time my preconceived ideas about the world were so fully challenged. Before understanding nonself, I had accepted much of what I had been taught to value in my Western upbringing. Once I grasped it, I hadn't learned just one idea, but thrown open the doors to entirely new ways of thinking and imagining. I began to understand that everything I thought was True or Real was just that: a belief. Afterward, through realizing that the way I imagined even something as elemental as my ideas about my "self" were up for debate, I came to understand that I *chose* to believe in each of the things I accepted as Truth. Therefore, if I trained my mind to believe differently, I could choose to experience the world in a completely new way. This was true intellectual and emotional freedom, not to mention responsibility: if I had the power to choose, then I truly was the architect of my life . . . I was the one responsible for every twist and turn, every life-changing belief. Afterward, I was not the same person, and never again would be.

Change is difficult.
Even when change is direly necessary, such as what is required of us by climate change, or the ending of a toxic relationship, we tend to steel ourselves against it with the entirety of our being. This is because we are more comfortable in the familiar; the familiar is something our emotional bodies will fight tooth and nail to retain.

Yet change is necessary for progress—for many, *this is the role of education.*

Putney, Morris & Sargent (2015)[17] posit that authentic learning *requires* change, and that it is only through experiencing the state of *discomfort* that accompanies change that we are able to truly experience its transformative power. The feeling of discomfort *is* change. That's what it feels like to uproot familiar belief systems and supplant them with new learning. This is what happens when change takes place.

Putney, Morris & Sargent call this state of discomfort "disequilibrium," and explain that contrary to what we might think, "when students feel totally at ease and comfortable . . . they are probably not learning." They go on to say that because of this, it is the challenge of all teachers to create "just the right amount of disequilibrium," a level of discomfort that is just disorienting enough to effectively "motivate students to integrate and comprehend" the knowledge being presented. The trick is to find a level of discomfort that is not so terrible that they will want to give up, categorizing the information as *too* difficult, but a level of discomfort that is manageable. A manageable level of discomfort is seen as a precursor to deep learning. This is a concept echoed by critical race scholars who work to help students face the ways that they are privileged and oppressed in current societal structures; in the difficult dialogues I have participated in, facilitators often state up front that getting uncomfortable is a core requirement for participation.[18] Without discomfort, there will not be the kind of inner growth we can proudly call "learning."

St. Mary's is not the only university where I experienced transformative change, but every time it happened, I can say definitely that two main ingredients were always present: 1) disequilibrium, and 2) a high level of trust between teacher and student.

For disequilibrium to work, an environment of care and comfort is essential. Had I not felt comfortable with my professors and the school environment that surrounded me, I would not have had the confidence to dig so deeply into my learning, allowing for a period of frustration and disorientation.

Educators committed to transformative change for their students need to foster classroom environments where students and teachers are able to safely have difficult conversations. They need to elevate students' voices so that they feel confident enough to engage in the class emotionally and spiritually as well as intellectually, and they need to foster trust in their students, who will look to them as a guide through their discomfort. This means treating students with respect and valuing their individual experiences as important. It also means engaging in thoughtful classroom discussions, and encouraging students to make their learning personal— whether it is a history class or an engineering practicum, student–teacher trust and personalized learning are always an option.

> **Jing:** We are challenged to "edu-care," to care for nature and for each other. In Chinese, the word "education" means *educate and foster, educate and bring up, educate and nurture, educate and transform,* and this involves pouring our energy of the heart, mind, and spirit into the process of learning, so that we grow love and light and great vision; in Chinese, this means seeking enlightenment for Dao.

Statistically, we (Amanda and Jing) are lucky.

The National Center for Education Statistics in the United States reports that only about 43 percent of high school graduates attend four-year universities after high school, and 20 percent attend two-year institutions.[19] According to UNESCO and the World Bank, the global percentage is nearly the same, hovering around 40 percent in 2021 (varying enormously by country).[20] Beyond the fact that I (Amanda) was able to attend a university at all, I also feel lucky to have had the support of my parents in choosing a small liberal arts school without an international reputation. I was not pushed to engage with education as a means to an end; rather, I was encouraged to see education as an end in itself, and to enjoy my learning as a journey. Since then, through the stories of students and friends who spent their junior year of high school in SAT Prep-courses, anxiously competing for the highest grades in the class, I know this experience is far from universal.

What can we do to make these experiences a realistic option for more people?

Jing: I also have parents who respect whatever decision I make and whatever passion I have. When I was little, I had such a thirst for learning that whenever I laid my hand on a book, I would plunge into it. I read Plato's Republic and Aristotle's Metaphysics although I could not understand anything; I read Chinese classics in prints that were incredibly tiny and went from top to bottom and were written in the most difficult ancient language; I read forbidden novels under the cover of a blanket as they were deemed "bad" by the society then: For all these things, my parents never stopped me or scolded me. Instead, they gave me a "lavish" allowance (one yuan each month) from their meager salary (58 yuan supporting seven people) every month, making me feel so rich (the amount is equivalent to hundreds of dollars a month today) and allowing me to buy books of various kinds. This was an incredible privilege, which I continued later on—I gave my children a handsome allowance and let them decide what to do with it. I was allowed to follow my passion and be who I am. My parents' unconditional love became the propelling force for me to learn a lot, continuously.

Universities as Transformative Change-Makers

A history of the university is beyond the scope of these pages, but throughout time they have been looked to as a way to educate the masses for the betterment of society. Over the years they have become bastions of thought, financing academics to lead the way in imagining, then implementing, brave new ideas with the support of the excited, energized youth that populate their hallways. As we enter this new stage of development, where the infrastructure of our global society threatens the future of our planet, and activists are calling for a total reimagination of the way we live, it makes sense that universities would be integral to the process.

Mark Stewart, once Sustainability Manager at the University of Maryland, said, "people around the world are looking to institutions of higher education to create sustainable solutions to our societal and technical challenges and to model a new era of living within our means."[21] In 2006, twelve college and university presidents initiated the American College and University President's Climate Commitment (ACUPCC). By 2007 more than 350 universities had made the pledge to "mobil[ize] a diverse array of higher education institutions to act on bold climate commitments, to scale campus climate initiatives, and to create innovative climate solutions."[22] Signatories to ACUPCC's initiative must publicly agree that "carbon neutrality and resilience are extremely high priority areas of action for all institutions," and make a pledge to "lead the nation in these efforts."[23] They then choose from one of three possible commitments: 1) to provide a "systems approach to mitigating and adapting to a changing climate," or 2) "achieving carbon neutrality as soon as possible," or 3) adapting resilience measures for their university. The signatories continue to grow each year, and the network claims to have inspired nearly 4,000 greenhouse gas inventories and 600 Climate Action Plans with public accountability measures, including the publication of their targets, strategies, and progress.

> **Jing**: As I have previously mentioned, I started to teach the course on Ecological Ethics and Education after I embarked on meditation and felt, distinctly, my own connection with nature. I also mentioned a student who wrote a final paper envisioning sustainability endeavors in higher education. Mark Stewart was this student. It was during the course that Mark started to get faculty and students in the university to sign a petition to set up an Office of Sustainability on campus. He eventually went to work as a program manager in the office he began, and over the years he and his colleagues got the university to set up a sustainability fund, offer a sustainability minor, integrate sustainability education into new student orientation, and train more than 200 faculty to incorporate sustainability into their

curriculum. All the initiatives he outlined in the final envisioning paper he wrote for the class were fulfilled twelve years later. Today Mark works for the Maryland Department of the Environment. His story demonstrates the power of envisioning, followed by action and mobilization of like-minded people.

As Mark says in his article, universities are essentially small cities that can inspire others while teaching thousands of impressionable young students to respect their environment, live more sustainably, and get involved in the climate movement more deeply. Students at the University of Maryland can be proud to go to a university that has achieved 55 percent reduction in net greenhouse gas emissions (although 12% of this was achieved through purchasing carbon offsets), as well as a university that offers a minor in Sustainability Studies and has twenty-two green buildings certified as LEED Silver or above.[24] UMD is also "the research lead for the University Climate Change Coalition," which is a network of eighteen universities working to "help communities accelerate local climate action."[25]

Universities around the world are taking similar actions, like the students in Montreal who are not just greening their campus but also actively targeting politicians and policymakers who hesitate to address climate change.[26] And like the California State University of Los Angeles, which has developed the first Hydrogen Research and Fueling Facility able to directly sell hydrogen fuel—a fuel that emits water vapor as its only emission—to owners of electric vehicles.[27] Similarly exciting is the Tulane Nitrogen Reduction Challenge, a challenge from Tulane University, which offered a cash prize of one million dollars to the most promising research in service of reducing nitrogen runoff from farms into local waterways. This runoff creates "dead zones" in major bodies of water around the world, which severely impair fisheries and destabilize ecosystems.[28]

These are just a few of the exciting projects being spearheaded by universities, whose budgets for research and concentration of passionate, excited minds—continually energized by, and held accountable to, the unbridled passion and idealism of young people—represent an exciting place for pushing and implementing change. They have the freedom, as institutions of higher education (rather than private industry), to push for solutions outside of the current infrastructure. With the right leadership, and the continual influx of passionate young minds pushing for change, individual universities are big enough and loud enough to serve as beacons of forward-thinking action and sustainability, as well as examples for other institutions, not to mention for the infrastructure of our cities, states, and even—one day—the structure of a nation.

When reading about the energy and passion on university campuses, it is easy to get swept away with positive thinking. As Sarah Buttenwieser says in her article, *Greening the Ivory Tower,* creating sustainable universities with a strong emphasis on living in equilibrium with the earth can help "to shape the worldview of an entire generation." We can feel the possibility of affecting the world through students who will become the thinkers and leaders who will shape our future world. Change at this level feels like the kind of thing that can change hearts and minds. If universities actually move to offer sustainability elements in every major on every campus, as Mark Stewart proposes they should, or if one day a new federal requirement for funding is made that creates a mechanism for enshrining the challenge of climate change into the credo of the university system, we may see enormous shifts in possibility and potential. But it is important to remember the lessons of the past—while integrating sustainability into every university curriculum is a bold and beautiful idea, it is not enough to simply cover material. Teaching about the effects of pollution and the solutions that are possible in the future has already been shown to have little impact without the spiritual, and heart-centered growth that creates transformative learning. The link between greed, wealth accumulation, our current global economy, and issues like war, inequality, racism and the climate crisis must also be made clear . . .

We need students to understand that the change we need is not skin-deep, but structural, institutional, and cultural. And we need teachers who are doing the inner work, and truly passionate about change, to lead the charge.

> **Jing**: It is deeply troubling to see that university events still end up with a lot of plastics dumped into trash cans by the most educated people; it is even more troubling that the most "quick-minded" and "math-smart" kids are pouring their energy ferociously into a passion for making tons of money for the already very wealthy people (e.g., working for wealth management companies to double or triple the wealth of the wealthy in a short period of time) regardless of environmental destruction. The fundamentals of universities have not changed, and our societies (with companies that hire computer software students at a salary several times higher than that of a nurse or a teacher) still put very little

value on those that care for others and care for nature (such as park rangers who are paid notoriously low salaries).

Even if we manage to impart these big ideas in the right ways, the average university student stays on campus only for four years, and during that time most students exist in a bubble where they don't need to worry about money or bills. Many have parents who are taking care of their needs, or they are existing on scholarships, or even loans, which will not start to make trouble for them until they graduate. Once these students leave their campuses and get their first bills, their priorities will, inevitably, shift. They will begin to feel in their bones the very real draw toward a life that values material possessions . . . it will seem as if they have no choice but to value wealth accumulation, because how else can they afford their rent, start a family, and send their own kids to college?

They will begin to understand why environmentalism is often called an elitist issue, because people who need to make a living, pay bills, and put food on the table don't have the luxury of caring about whether or not a waterway in another part of the country or the world is in crisis. Or whether or not people in a community they have never been to and have never met are drinking and bathing in toxic water due to runoff from coal plants in their neighborhoods.[29] These students will be bombarded by a culture of greed, wealth accumulation, and false ideals of "success," which will quickly erode their dedication to environmentalism in pursuit of a life with the least difficulty and the most pleasure. This is why we need to do more than inspire students with ideas and information . . . we need them to *feel, with all of their hearts and whole bodies,* the *interconnection* of humans with the earth, and the link we share with *all* living beings.

We cannot settle for more funding or changes in the curriculum, because what we really need is a spiritual transformation . . . something that will not be easily shaken; something that will guide future generations to stay true to the values of sustainability, compassion, and love once they are beyond the university's influence. We need universities to influence future generations to demand change continually, over the course of their whole lives, even when the idealism of youth wanes, and the realities of the world settle in. This requires a rebalancing of logic with love; an integration of the mind-based, *yang* energy, which abounds in educational contexts, with the sensual, intuitive, *yin* energy, so that learning will not reside only in the minds of our students, but also in their hearts and whole bodies.

You might be wondering what kind of changes we would need to make on university campuses to achieve the transformative changes we need to address climate change. To this question, we throw out the following possibilities . . .

- What if we created sustainability education on college campuses where nature is incorporated into all of the curriculum?
- What if, as a part of their education, students were exposed to real life, emotionally resonating with consequences of the current global structures such as human suffering and environmental destruction?
- What if, instead of simply reading about the effects of industrialized agriculture in a textbook, they visited waterways where coal sludge is dumped and slaughterhouses where they faced the animals that they would eat?
- What if they engaged in exchange programs with neighborhoods different from their own economically, or did collaborative work with inmates in prisons?
- What if students from the suburbs spent a week in urban neighborhoods without grocery stores, businesses, or doctors' offices?

Students could then be asked to reflect on these things through meditation, journaling, attending lectures and visiting prisons, then talking to people who have these experiences. Many of these ideas are already being implemented in small liberal arts colleges, but they are nowhere near common.

> **Jing:** We cannot change unless our deepest feelings are transformed. Higher education must teach students to be true to their core being, to base their decisions in life in alignment with their values. Tom Culham (2013) has delved very deeply into how emotion is behind ethics in business decision-making. He talks about how our values and decisions are based on emotions, and emotions are connected to what we hold true; through meditation, we are more in touch with our inner value, which is connected to the Dao consciousness, where there is not an individual self, but everything is interconnected. It is through contemplative inquiry like meditation that we can tap into the deeper reality, the universal consciousness that connects all existence.

Suggested Reflective Activity #12: Considering the Possibilities of Education

We invite you to FREE WRITE on any or all of the following questions:

PART I:

1. Briefly describe your K-12 educational experience—was it traditional or non-traditional?

   a. What were the positive things about your education?
   b. What elements do you think could have been improved?

2. Do you believe something is missing from traditional education as it is practiced today?

   a. If so, why?
   b. If not, why?

3. Do you agree that K-12 learning should be transformed to be more engaged, holistic, and transformative for young minds?

   a. If so, what do you think could, or should, be changed?
   b. If not, why?

4. Do you think contemplative learning and/or democratic schooling has something important to offer to the future of education?

   a. If so, what?
   b. If not, why?

PART II:

1. If you went to university, how would you describe your experience?

2. Have you experienced disequilibrium in learning?

   a. If so, how was it created? What did you grapple with? Did it end in transformative learning? Why/why not?
   b. If not, can you point to anything about your educational experience that might have made this impossible?

3. What is the most supporting, nurturing learning environment you have experienced?

4. Do you agree that teachers in all disciplines, at all levels—from K-12 to university—are able to foster more engaged learning environments which not only nurture strong student–teacher relationships, but also lead to transformative change through a careful balance of love and disequilibrium?

   – What are the obstacles/challenges to creating this?
   – What would be the rewards?

PART III:

1. What do you believe is the role of universities in young people's lives today?
2. What do you believe *should be* the role of the university?
3. Do you agree that there is something unique to universities which makes engaged, holistic learning more feasible?

   – If so, what is it?

4. Do you agree that universities are an important place to activate younger generations and work toward change?

   – If so, what are some concrete steps you think universities should take?
   – If not, why?

5. How do you feel we could change college campuses so that they do not just educate, but also transform students' understanding of the climate crisis?
6. How do you feel we could better leverage educational institutions in general to ensure a more just, sustainable, and peaceful global society?

Act IV

"RESTORYING" FOR CHANGE
WHAT DOES IT MEAN AND HOW DOES IT WORK?
(A BEGINNER'S GUIDE)

Scene 9

THE POWER OF STORY
TOWARD AN UNDERSTANDING OF ITS ROLE IN OUR LIVES

Story plays a powerful and important role in our lives.

As our lives unfold, we narrate our experiences through an inner voice that frames them as meaningful stories—the story of how we became independent from our parents; the story of how we first fell in love; the story of who we are as professionals, friends, and lovers. We tell ourselves stories about our value and our worth. Stories about where we're from and what we're capable of. And we use, whether consciously or not, the power of storytelling to understand and make sense of our lives: our trauma, our joy, our travel, and so forth. Many psychologists and narrative researchers agree that what forms through this process of storying is nothing less than our concept of "self," our "I," which McAdams, Josselson, and Lieblich describe as our "narrative identity." Our narrative identity is inextricably linked to the inner voice we first hear as children, and the stories we tell ourselves (in this narrative voice) about what happens to us day after day.[1,2] As McAdams, Josselson, and Lieblich ask: "What is consciousness if not an inner narration of experience?" Taking that one step further, we may ask: Who is the "I," or "Me" in our minds, if not a collection of experiences we have formed into a whole through story?

Without our stories, who would we be?

If any one of our *core stories* were changed—the story of our family, the story of our track record of love, the story of our professional development—what key elements of our personality or beliefs would change along with them?

While we can't change the facts of our lives—that is, where we were born and how we were raised—what we *can* do is take ownership over the autobiographical narrating voice that brings meaning to these stories and choose to frame our stories in purposeful ways.

In other words, if we want to change ourselves—if we want to change our *reality*—one place to start is with the stories we live and tell every day.[3]

Stories About Ourselves and Others

Recently, as a newcomer in Taipei, I have been meeting a lot of new people.

As we sit down to a coffee or a beer, facing one another across the round table of a coffee shop or touching shoulders on a sofa, what we naturally find ourselves doing is swapping the most important stories of our lives, taking the other person on a guided tour of who we are through story. As I tell these stories, I notice that I pick and choose, edit, re-form, and reframe the stories I tell to suit the audience I am with, and the version of my "self" I am willing to share at that time.

For me—and likely for you—there are a few central stories from my life experience that carry particular, formative weight. If I want to get close to someone, these are the stories I know I will eventually share, because without knowing these the other person will not have a true picture of who I am. These include the story of my early twenties, when I left the United States for Taiwan and ended up staying in Asia for nearly six years, reckless and young, full of ignorance and privilege, in love and full of adventure. Perhaps I will tell you about my time at Greenpeace, hanging banners for the climate, or trips I have taken. If I feel close to the person, I might choose to trust them with honest stories of deep friendship, love, loss, and learning.

After story-swapping with someone new, what the other person really *knows* about me is dependent on the way I frame the stories I share. If I frame myself as a freedom-loving hero or a daring girl; if I choose to weave in the difficult pieces, like depression, weight gain, and self-doubt; or if I summarize without delving too deeply. These choices say a lot about who I think I am and who I am trying to be. They also say a lot about my level of comfort or interest in the other person. After story-swapping, as I walk back to my apartment or my car, I will probably tell myself a story about the experience we shared, which categorizes it in some way—do I feel closer to that person now? Connected? Intimate? In love? Did I feel *seen* and *heard*? Or misunderstood and ignored? Was I eager to leave, and relieved to be alone? Or hesitant to part ways?

Whatever my takeaway, it is the way I choose to frame that conversation in my mind, and the way I then *tell the story* of that conversation to others, which will determine my level of commitment to a relationship with that person in the future. The next time I see them, or think of them, my eagerness to invest more or pull back will be based on the foundation laid by the stories I told in my mind.

This is the power of my inner narrating voice.

Suggested Reflective Activity #13: The Stories We Tell

We are constantly telling stories about ourselves and the people in our lives, the tone and tenor of which is decided by what we choose to share or not at the time. We can see this clearly in interviews, where we are tasked with constructing stories about ourselves as workers; or on dates, where we task ourselves with constructing a story that presents us in a desirable way. Internally, and with our loved ones, we tell stories about the things we have done, which brings meaning to those experiences, solidifying them in our minds. This Reflective Activity is designed to help us explore this more deeply, considering the ways story has presented itself in our personal lives.

**We invite you to FREE WRITE on any or all of the
following questions:**

1. Consider the last time you met someone new and had a conversation that included the work of "getting to know" one another . . .

   a. What did you share about yourself? Why?
   b. What did you leave out? Why?
   c. What did you learn about the other person that stays with you still?

2. Now consider the last time you spoke to someone who left a big impression on you, whether positive or negative.

   a. When you look back on that conversation and consider explaining it to another person, what will you say?
   b. What impression will the story you tell leave—both on the person you tell it to, and in your own memory?
   c. Now consider "restorying" that interaction in a different way—how easy would it be to change the feeling of the experience by retelling it in a different way? Focusing on different details, and framing them in a different way?

3. Would you say that you are aware of the power of story in
   your life, consciously shaping stories to create the meaning or
   impression you prefer them to have? Or are you at the mercy of
   your inner narrating voice?

From Understanding to Agency

Understanding how we construct and tell our stories can help give us
agency and ownership over the meaning of their plotlines.

Narrative researchers agree that we are constantly collecting
experiences that create our shifting inner worlds, just as discourse
theorists find that we are constantly positioning ourselves with others
in particular ways (whether consciously or unconsciously) and being
forcibly positioned by others.[4] We coalesce these various experiences
into the expression of one single (albeit continually developing),
central, internally formed narrative, which represents our idea of
"self."[5] Interestingly, research has found that our personal stories
include many traditional characteristics and structures, such as a
setting, character types, and narrative arc (or plot).[6]

The setting for our stories may include obvious elements of place
and time, as well as less obvious structural elements, like the (often
invisible) cultural, familial, and societal stories in which we are raised.[7]
These may include stories about gender, race, class, and ability that we
have internalized as "normal," or cultural stories we have absorbed over
time about what makes a "good life" or an "honorable" person.[8] They
may also include the personal ideologies and systems of belief in which
we are raised, such as big-picture philosophical beliefs about how the
world was created and the meaning of life, or smaller philosophies about
the best way to make a friend or carry on a conversation. Alongside our
philosophies are our political beliefs, big and small, such as whether
war is an acceptable way to settle disputes and if the environment is
worth sacrificing, whether for convenience or for money. These are
further complicated by localized political beliefs about things like race,
class, and spending.

Whatever our personal system of beliefs, taken together they form
an ideology that not only contributes to who we are but also leads us
into (and out of) certain relationships and life-experiences. In this way,
our personal ideologies contribute to the formation of a certain kind
of life—will you prefer to stay in the town where you grew up, or move

to a new place? Will you create meaningful friendships across cultures and linguistic barriers? Will you seek out adventure? Or will you prefer to stay wrapped in the sweet comfort of the familiar, prioritizing depth over breadth? Regardless of what your beliefs are, they are in part responsible for the choices you make, which of course plays an enormous role in the stories we live and tell, and the life we create.[9]

Researchers have found both traditional character types and a sense of plot in our personal stories. The characters we shape include the familiar, culturally embedded tropes of hero, villain, and victim that, once formed, carry extraordinary power in our lives and minds.[10] The characters we form then act out their roles along an inwardly formed narrative arc, or sense of plot, which includes a beginning, middle, and endpoint, as well as moments of rising and falling action, such as when our personal narrative intersects with or diverges from the narratives of others, creating moments of friendship and romance, as well as conflict and rejection.[11]

The beauty of this way of seeing and being is that who we are is constantly being negotiated and renegotiated through our autobiographical narrator's voice—when each new experience is framed by a story, then with each story we tell there is an opportunity to *story ourselves* into a new way of thinking and being. As such, we have both the power and opportunity to identify the stories that hold us back, and *restory* those in ways that serve us. In support of restorying with intention and purpose, knowing what we want—a change or goal we desire—will act as a guiding light in the dark.

A Look at the Evidence: Ways Storytelling Creates Change

There is powerful evidence in the field of healthcare and psychotherapy that personal narratives—and the powerful act of *restorying* those narratives—can be used to create positive change. Narratives are identified as a useful tool because of the ability of a narrative to create a strong emotional connection in our hearts and minds. Every good storyteller knows that when a narrative's main characters elicit compassion or love from the listener, and the plot creates a sense of drama or tension which makes the listener care about what will happen, the result is that the listener becomes immersed in the story—fully lost in the world they have entered, utterly attentive.

Hinyard and Kreuter describe this state as *absorption*, noting that when listeners are *absorbed* in a story their resistance is lowered, and the likelihood that they will accept the message of the narrative is increased.¹² They explain that narratives have been successfully used to teach life-saving skills to healthcare workers, such as problem-solving and decision-making while in emergencies. They have also been used to model healthy behavior for the prevention of HIV/AIDS, and to communicate the effectiveness of mammograms for identifying breast cancer before it metastasizes. When the target message is communicated through the techniques and components of a narrative (such as character and plot), changes in the listener are more likely to occur, underscoring the importance of engaging with the traditional narrative components of a story in our personal change-making work.

One particularly successful and well-known organization that leverages stories to create significant and meaningful change is Alcoholics Anonymous. Alcoholics who engage in the program have been shown to come away with "increased self-efficacy, greater commitment to abstinence, greater acceptance of an alcoholic identity, and increased social support" through the shared experience of storytelling.¹³ One important element of the program is community-building, which is done through the *telling of* and *listening to* personal stories in a group setting. Facilitators use the group storytelling experience to model essential elements of relationship-building (sharing and listening), which in turn creates a strong community of support for participants. An enormous benefit of AA's group modeling is that it is able to offer participants examples of stories they can take for themselves, exposing them to plots and themes that *restory* the shared experience of alcoholism as destructive and shameful into an inspirational story of recovery. Waters describes the work of reframing and restorying as a kind of "autobiographical reconstruction" which, when successful, creates a new sense of identity underscored by the "broader story of the AA program."

The change that Alcoholics Anonymous (AA) members experience centers around the claiming of a *new story* and a *new identity* through storytelling. While the community is an important element of AA, participants interviewed about the program highlight the simple act of *telling* their story, whether to others or simply in a diary, as especially transformative. They explain that this act "allow[ed] for a sense of meaning to emerge from what was experienced in the moment as senselessness, helplessness, and despair," underscoring the relationship between what we experience and the way we frame these experiences through story. This sort of telling, whether to an actual other or an imagined one, helps us to "understand ourselves better as we tell," and this practice of telling our stories to others we believe (or imagine) are witnesses, helps us to create our sense of self, and, later, to heal that self. From the perspective of a contemplative educator concerned with educating the whole being, we might also interpret this experience of *storying meaning* as evidence of the impact personal stories have on our spiritual and emotional beings.

The work of creating personal change through story is underscored by therapists and psychotherapists who help their clients by first encouraging the telling of their client's stories, then finding ways for their clients to take ownership of their narrative voice, intentionally re-framing difficult stories in positive and empowering ways. Angus and Hardtke conducted an analysis of one client's stories in order to showcase the process of "narrative story change in psychotherapy."[14] Through this process, they identified three elements of storytelling that are always at work in each storyteller:

1) the external narrative process, or the stories we tell other people about what we feel, believe, and know;
2) the internal narrative process, or the way our stories are understood by us internally—in our bodies, our hearts, and minds, and so forth; and
3) the reflexive narrative process, or the process of interpreting our narratives and assigning meaning to them.

Angus and Hardtke explain that we succeed in changing meaning-making when we learn to purposefully and clearly shift *from* the reactive, uncritical mode of simply *telling* stories that arise in us naturally (the external storytelling mode), *to* differentiating internally between the stories we are telling and the experiences we are having. Once we are able to differentiate between what we feel and the stories we tell, we gain power over our emotions. In other words, once we are able to pause between the feeling of an emotion and the telling of a story that justifies it, successfully divorcing our emotions from the power of its adjoining narrative, we gain the ability to look at our stories as constructions and our emotions as self-made. Doing this helps us to gain a sense of agency over our stories and, by proxy, our emotions. If we change the stories we tell, we can change what we believe and feel. If we have the power to change what we believe and feel, we have the power to change a great many things about who we are now and what we are capable of being.

If we want to change the way we are in the world, if we want to transform our daily living *away from* the consumerist, commercialist, and unsustainable living practices considered the "norm" in American society and move *toward* peace and harmony with the environment, our internal personal stories are a great place to start. Simply put . . . if we want to change the way we are in the world, we need to learn to tell a different story. The good news is that our personal stories *are something each one of us has control over.* While change is never easy, storytelling, at least, can be fun.

From the research presented here, we have learned a great deal about the ingredients needed for a powerful, change-making story. We know that

1. for a story to create change, it needs to *absorb* us emotionally.
2. for a story to evoke emotion, it must have narrative characteristics, such as a beginning, a middle, and an end, as well as a plot, scene, characters, conflict, and so on.
3. the *telling* of these stories—internally, to ourselves, and out loud, to friends, family, and perhaps even larger communities—is part of what gives us the agency to take on a new autobiographical identity.
4. changing our internal stories means understanding the connection between the stories we tell and the emotions we feel, then stepping in to disassociate from our knee-jerk stories so that we can then tell a new story that better serves us.

Suggested Reflective Activity #14: Exercising Agency

We invite you to FREE WRITE on any or all of the following questions:

PART I: Personal Stories and the Power of Purposeful Framing

1. Think about some of the personal narratives you hold in your heart about particularly memorable experiences in your life. Don't overthink or edit as you consider your stories—consider the stories you hold in your arsenal and tell regularly.
   Now try the following:

   a. Summarize one of the stories you hold that frames you in a positive light.
   b. Summarize one of the stories you tell that frames you in a negative light.

2. Try flipping one, or both, of the stories you've just summarized—rewrite the positive story in a negative light, or (this will be more fun) rewrite the negative story in a positive light!
3. Reflect on this experience of purposeful reframing—was it Easy? Difficult? Why?

PART II: Storying the Environmental Crisis

Let's consider the stories you tell yourself about the environmental crisis and your role in it. To get you started, try finishing the following sentences with personal stories:

a) My primary story about the environmental crisis is:
b) My primary story intersects with the global cultural story of money and markets by:
c) One way I could reframe my story about the environmental crisis is:

PART III: Storying Myself as an Environmental Actor

Now let's consider the stories you tell yourself about your agency and power as a change-maker in this movement, toward a more just and sustainable future. To get you started, try finishing the following sentences with personal stories:

a) One of the stories I tell myself to justify unsustainable practices in my life is:
b) I tell myself this story because:
c) One way that I could reframe this story is:

Scene 10

A NEW NARRATIVE BEGINNING
STORYING YOURSELF INTO A COURAGEOUS FORCE FOR CHANGE

We have finally arrived . . .
Not to the end, but the beginning—
    The beginning of a new way of thinking, being and knowing . . .
    . . . . the beginning of a new story.

To help you on your journey of restorying, we have decided to leave you with a suggested narrative opening, one that we hope will both capture your imagination and inspire your first steps.

Please read this suggested opening as a gift and a possibility. As something for you to take and use. To meditate on and believe in. Or *re*think and *re*tell in your own words, with your own sense of place, character, and scene.

Regardless of how you read these words, and whatever they may come to mean, remember to open your heart as you read and listen with your whole being.

Before you begin, take a moment to make sure you are in a comfortable place where you will not be disturbed.

Perhaps you will want to curl up with a blanket or a cup of something exciting.

If you are able, find a place where you can see the natural world—from a window, from a back porch, maybe even outside, sitting in a park or wild place. If it's not possible for you to sit with a view of nature, then imagine the natural world in your mind. Feel the warmth of the sun on your skin, a gentle breeze, the energy of all living things cup you warmly.

Now, take a few long, deep breaths.

Let the air come into your lungs and flow through your whole body.

As it comes out, feel yourself relax.

Do this as many times as you need to let the stress of the day melt from your skin, letting any anxiety or worry simply slip away.

Once you are comfortable and fully relaxed, open yourself to the powerful energy of the world, which is always around you. Feel its loving embrace. Feel it smile inside you generously.

When you're ready, read the narrative beginning we have written with a lightness of being that is open to possibility. Let its energy take shape however you need.

Let it flow into your being, inspiring your emotional and spiritual bodies, scintillating your mind, rising like a tide in the womb of every cell, flowing like a powerful river through every capillary . . .

A Narrative Beginning

Imagine, for a moment, that you are a child.

Not in body, but in elasticity of belief; in openness of heart; and newness of understanding.

Believe, with the surety of your entire being—in the same way that you *know* that you will not float up to the ceiling today, and that your bones will not collapse into dust while you're still breathing—**believe**, from the tips of your fingers to the warm bend of skin beneath your knees, that your mind is a truly unparalleled, wondrous, powerful thing. That the narratives you live and tell, the "self" you form, and the world you *story* into being, have the power to tear down what does not serve you and create a brand-new beginning.

Now take another deep breath. As you breathe in, imagine you are breathing in the power to create the world in which you live.

As you breathe out, feel all the beliefs and stories that do not serve you slipping from your body.

If it feels right, do this a few more times, and each time you breathe in let the power of possibility fill you completely. Each time you breathe out, let all the old, stale air, and all the storylines of negativity and helplessness that stop you from living a life of courage and action flow from you easily, as if your body is cleansing itself of what does not serve it, becoming pure and warm, bathing in a buttery yellow light.

Once you are fully relaxed, imagine you are walking the last few feet of a long, winding path through a familiar forest. You have been walking for a long time, through all kinds of weather and all times of day. As you walked, your path was consistently shaded by an arched canopy of interlocking branches that pull your attention upward now, toward the sky. You marvel at the watercolor of browns, yellows, and reds above you, at the birds singing in the puzzle of wood that protected you when it stormed and shaded you from the powerful rays of the sun in the middle of the day. You are grateful for the leaves that cover the dirt beneath your feet, and for the flowers and treesthat bloom in every inch of the forest, reminding you of the intricately woven miracle of life.

Before you now, you can see the edge of the forest, where the path opens up into a sea of unshaded green. Excited, you hurry your feet. As you emerge there is the warmth of the late afternoon sun on your face. A breeze starts from somewhere far away, streams gently toward you, lifts your hair from the temples and rustles your shirtsleeves. Your legs are tired from the long journey, and this feels like a wonderful place to sit and rest.

At the edge of the path, just on the other side of the trees, you lower yourself on a circle of yellow-green grass and stretch out your legs.

You breathe in, noticing the sweetness of lemon and honeysuckle on your tongue.

You breathe out, feeling the powerful lungs of so many friendly trees at your back, in quiet sync.

As you breathe in again, you close your eyes, and when you open them you are greeted by a magical carpet of bountiful grassland. Its many shades of green and brown and blue twinkle as the clouds pass between the sun and the land. You feel the busy hum of living things moving this way and that. You blink at the wondrous sight, sweeping your gaze from one end of the rolling green fields to the other. Wildflowers tilt their heads. Deer drop their necks. Insects cut zigzag paths between the twining grass. You see that a long river, like a ribbon of blue, snakes through the fields to your left, and a sparkling half-moon lake sits proud and full to your right. The wind blows, rustling the grass and enlivening the animals, so that the whole long stretch of living beings seem to lift their voices and sing with one voice.

Beyond the grassland, off in the distance, you see another forest of interlocking trees. Beyond the trees, so far away from you now that it is like the smoothed flat of turquoise glass, is the sea. It is clean and clear, slipping from turquoise blue to jade green to marble white. In some places you can see the brightness of the sky reflected in the glassy surface, while in other places waves rise and fall, their foamed tips crashing playfully against one another.

The enormity of what is before you takes shape, a reminder of what is possible in this life. Its song swims through your arms and legs, a river of wisdom connecting you to a deep knowing, something you know has been in you always, but which can be difficult to hear when you are moving through the ups and downs of your day.

Now, as you sit, calm and present in its midst, you are able to watch and listen easily to its divine voice. You know, in the part of you that has always been in touch with the wisdom of the world, that you are one with this place: its complex wholeness; its interconnected, endless weave of living energy; its profound mosaic of unconditional love and beauty for anyone to enjoy. You know this universe of energy as you know your own body, because you are as much a part of these powerful layers of birth and death, and the careful balance it keeps, as every other living thing. This profound sense of recognition and belonging whispers excitedly in your mind, swims through your heart, and dances in your spirit, calling for you to take your rightful place.

As you sit and gaze out on this family of living beings you realize that you know, in your bones, a truth: you are not separate from the exquisite artistry of the world at your feet. It is around you and inside you always. It is something you have always felt—in the quiet whispers of the wind as you sat by water, in the magical blink of fireflies in summer, in the faint twinkle of the stars as you gazed at the sky—that every living thing, including the rolling green fields before you, the thick canopy of twisted branches at your back, and the sparkling water in the distance, are not something separate or apart, but a home for your spirit. You are interconnected and interlinked. Not above or below, but in your very source of life . . . in the vital energy that connects every living thing, which runs through your body as well as theirs.

As you sit with this knowing, your heart fills with the pride of belonging, bringing you warmth and peace.

You close your eyes and take a long breath in, filling your body.

Hold that breath in your chest. Feel it extend to your stomach. Listen as it runs happily through your arms and legs.

As you let it out, feel your body lighten and release.

As you sit, give thanks. Bow your head and smile at the renewal of your energy.

You would like to stay, but there is a knowing nudge at the bottom of your belly, a plea from your Earth-family, because these places will not remain wild or untouched much longer if you and I don't do something.

There is peace and balance here, in this place; but nearby there are oceans, rivers, mountains, and grasslands in terrible pain. You can feel their confusion and terror in the whole of your body. They choke on polluted water and air. They watch their human brothers and sisters in disbelief. The weight of their struggle is a call for help, which you are eager to meet—you know that it does not take a miracle, or any kind of superpower to do the right thing. What is needed is for people to simply open their eyes and remember how to see.

The fight will be long and difficult. Full of ignorance and greed. But the strength they offer you now is an ancient one, birthed by the universe itself, as old as time.

Its endlessness and possibility are a deep, guttural, ancestral thing, and you feel its resolve taking shape in your bones, becoming stronger and deeper with each breath you take.

You open to it without question and it fills you completely. Like a hand on your shoulder or a wind at your back. Like a friend wrapping their arms around your body.

You feel its wisdom seep through your skin, into your blood, pumped by your own heart, glowing with energy, lighting up your muscles and organs from the inside.

The strength that is spreading through you now is the strength and wisdom of every living thing that has come before, every unborn thing yet to come, and all things alive today. This powerful community settles inside you, waiting.

You put your hands on the grass, plant your feet on the ground, and stand, feeling the powerful muscles of your legs, the mightiness of your breath, the enduring promise of so much loving energy.

As you stand you raise your arms from your sides, reach your hands to the air, and pull in one last breath of cleansing energy—you have known for as long as you have been alive that something is coming. That there is a darkness in this world that seeks out wild places. A blindness in people who have forgotten how to reach out their hands and cup the water or wind with their whole being.

But *you* are here now, with your heart and spirit open to the world, full of the loving kindness that has shaped you into the friend they need— you will not turn your back on your family. You will be courageous and steady in the face of the change we need.

This feeling of oneness—this knowledge of your fluid interconnection with every living thing—*this* is what has brought you here. At this time, to this place. It is what positions you to stand at the precipice of our world with this promise in your body.

You are animated now, refreshed and bold with decision, vibrating with a lithe, spirited energy that overflows into the welcoming world. It is as if the living world has felt your promise, and is reaching out to you with gratitude and a promise of its own—to be with you always.

You see it in the wink of the water as it swims in the sun.

You feel it in the caress of the wind against your face.

You nod your head and agree—*you, for your part, are ready!*

Not just to open yourself to the gifts around you, but to *speak* their words and *give them a voice.*

A laugh escapes from your lips as you suddenly understand that *this* is why you came—not just to remember who you are or what is at stake, but to experience how *right* it feels to decide, with every ounce of power in your body, to stand with the world and commit to be a champion in this fight!

You feel as if you could hold your ground before all the world's ignorance and greed, knowing that the shared foundation of love that flows through you now will easily outlast the flimsiness of material things.

You have the living world at your back!

Its ancient wisdom rises like a tide in your animal-heart, taking root in your mind, spirit, and body.

You are teeming with wisdom, overflowing with love, and full of an otherworldly grace! You know now what you came here to remember:

You are powerful and unafraid.

Your strength is whole and endless in the face of the world's darkest decision, because you are more than one being! You are more than one body! You are the totality of the Earth and all her creatures. You are the mountains, the streams, the rivers, and the forests—all of these reside in your body.

Like the Earth and all her creatures, you are capable and stalwart, determined to find a way.

You feel yourself taking shape . . .

You are a warrior for love.

A mighty force for justice.

You feel the smile in your gut before it forms on your lips.

Before it gently transforms what remains in your body of doubt and hesitation into courage, determination, and pride.

Your spirit is light and alive with the promise you have made.

Your reward is not some far away memory or distant place; it is the preservation of your home—*our* home—and the promise of balance, safety, and peace.

As you survey the expanse of brown and red and green, the flow of air and water, the rip of wind through the trees, you are grateful for the knowledge that every living thing is in you always. Your animal family.

No one has ever been more ready. No one has ever been better positioned or full of determination, courage, and wisdom.

And so you turn back from the edge of the Earth to face in the other direction. Toward the path you came along, back to the world you left behind.

You put your arms out wide and raise them to the sky.

You let out a battle cry that is quickly mirrored and matched, in tone and tenor, with what you know now is an army of people spread out across the great expanse of the Earth, each and every one filled with so much determination that the air around you crinkles and cracks with their commitment.

You are side by side, shoulder to shoulder, with an ocean of people just like you, full of optimism and faith. Stubbornness and pride. Love and hope. The courage of the ages.

We are, all of us, inexhaustible and determined.

This knowledge expands in your chests and reverberates through your arms, legs, and heart.

Each one of us standing on this precipice now knows that we have no choice.

The world is in danger and *we* are the only ones who can save it.

There is no *later.*

There is no *tomorrow.*

The fight has been going on long before this moment, and there is no other time in the world to act but *now,* in *our lives,* and then outward and onward forever.

We know that it will be difficult for the world to change.

People will be angry, full of spite and greed and hateful language, but we are not scared of how hard it will be or how long it will take.

We are not scared of what might happen along the way; it will be much more difficult to remain inactive, or to wait. And so we would rather run into the danger with our eyes open than lie down and let what is coming have its way.

The journey before us now is bigger than you or me.

It is bigger than any one person.

This is the battle of our lifetime—the battle of all the living generations.

If we win, we will have saved our home . . . our human and nonhuman family.

If we lose, we will have allowed the planet that sustains us to buckle beneath our weight, forcing it to transform *away* from human life.

This knowledge fills us with superhuman strength.

Time is running out and there is no more time to waste!
We reach out across time and space.
We grip hands with our family, human and nonhuman alike.
We raise our voices in song, set our sights at the target before us, and take off running . . .

Jing:
> A tipping point will come when enough people let go of fear and join the force for change – for a better, more sustainable world, where Mother Earth is in us and we are in her. Where we recognize that we are her children Where we are grateful and humble, joining joyously in the cosmic dance of life, ascending to our higher spiritual landscape by embodying unconditional Love for all of existence . . . for all living beings. Let us be the change, starting Now!

(Final) Reflective Activity #15: Claiming Your Narrative Voice

We invite you to FREE WRITE on any or all of the following questions:

PART I: Reflecting on the Narrative Beginning just described

1. Reflect on the narrative you just read: how does it feel in your body? Does it feel right for you? Can you use it to *story* yourself into a powerful character capable of achieving great change?

2. What can you change about your life today, or this week (or this year), to help you live out a new story of courage, determination, and love for nature?

PART II: Writing your own Narrative Beginning

The story we left you with is meant to inspire and provoke a new beginning. To underscore the central values of belief, courage and determination that are needed as you take your first steps into a new character's shoes. But it is only one of many possible beginnings— ultimately, you are a unique and beautiful soul. As such, you must choose your own path. You must do the work in your own life, in your own way, that leads to transformative moments of heart-based and spiritual change.

Now find a journal or something to write in, and take the time to form your own narrative beginning. Perhaps you will want to write something completely new and fully your own; or perhaps you would like to use our narrative beginning as a starting point. Either way, before you begin, answer the following questions about who you want to be in the fight to come—

- What character will you inhabit?
- What actions will you take?
- Where will you place your feet and take your stand?

Before you begin, take a few deep breaths—long inhales with your eyes closed, slow and controlled exhales with your eyes at half-mast.

Let in the loving energy around you.

Let it flow through your whole being.

Let it smile in your heart.

Feel its smile in your stomach, chest, and back.

Feel it tickling at the corners of your lips.

Imagine yourself as a courageous and powerful soul capable of creating the change we need. Where are you? What do you hear, see, taste, and smell? Who is there at your side, to inspire and work alongside you?

What voice will you inhabit? What words will you speak? What actions will you take? And where will you go?

With these questions in your mind, and the spirit of loving energy in your heart, pick up your pen, and write your story . . .

Epilogue:

Thank you for joining us on this journey of reflection and story.

We hope you have found inspiration in these pages. Above all, we hope that you have begun to consider ways to **reimagine** and **restory** your relationship with the natural world in ways that make you feel powerful and courageous in the face of changes we need, and the sacrifices that wait. It is our belief that the reason we (humans) have allowed the planet to come so dangerously close to catastrophic climate change is a spiritual imbalance, both with ourselves and the natural world. Within ourselves, we have privileged the logical mind over all other ways of thinking and being, which has led to a lack of emotional and spiritual understanding. Without the great wisdom of our emotional and spiritual bodies, our knowledge is incomplete. As a result, we look at the natural world—its magical bounty, its dying animals and plants, its old growth trees—and mistakenly see them as separate from ourselves, or unworthy of the same love and respect we would offer our own families. We continue to look at them and see "resource" or "beautiful place," when what we should be seeing is "home" and "spirit" and "family." What we fail to understand is that with every animal we tear from its home, every old growth forest we clear-cut, every mountain we remove, every stream, river, and ocean we dump our unwanted waste into, we are not only destroying the only home we have ever known but also losing pieces of ourselves along the way. As we sign papers and collect money and continue on this path of heartless "development," we are losing sight of the planet that sustains us. Every time we turn our heads from the carnage, we travel further from our heart and spirit bodies, distorting our connection with the great love and wisdom of the universe that gave us life.

In this book we have tried to offer several ways of thinking, knowing, and understanding as tools for creating the change we need. These include meditation; walks in nature; alternative philosophical and spiritual approaches to knowing, such as yin/yang, and inter-being; alternative models of education, such as contemplative education and democratic schooling; as well as an array of inspirational and provocative stories collected from our (Amanda and Jing's) own personal experience. Ultimately, we hope we have made clear that what is needed in this moment, and for a long time to come, is **belief** in yourself as a powerful force, **courage** to face the obstacles in our path, and **determination** to stay the course. Without these things we will languish in the in-between space of inaction and denial; with these things, there is the bright, glorious moon of hope to guide our way.

The main tool we have offered for your journey toward a more courageous actor in the fight for change is story. We believe that story is at the very foundation of who we are—it is how we understand and give meaning to our experiences. It is also how we animate ourselves and all living things. Understanding the power it has through inherited cultural, corporate, and philosophical stories, deepened and propagated further by schools and media, is its own kind of weapon. The thing to know is this: *you don't need to accept the story you have been given.* Rather, the story you live is in great part determined by the ownership you choose to take over your own narrative voice, and the way you use that voice to tend and shape your inner and outer world. We hope that this book has inspired you to take note of the stories that surround you and consider them as material to fashion as you like—they are not "the truth"; they are not any sort of predetermined end. They are only stories in which you play a role; your end within each tale is determined by no one else but you.

Remember that it does not matter where you have been, or what you have done before this day. What matters is this . . .

Given what you know about the state of the world and what it needs, from this day forward, what story will you live and tell? Who will you choose to be?

We hope you will tell a story of balance and inter-being. A story of power and hope. A story that helps you face the difficult challenge ahead with power, determination, and courage.

Take ownership over your narrative voice in the way that feels right to you.

Find your own balance and your own peace.

Tell your own story.

Thank you for traveling with us on this journey!

NOTES

Introduction

1 Lew, D. N. M., & Schmidt, H. G. (2011). Writing to learn: Can reflection journals be used to promote self-reflection and learning? *Higher Education Research & Development, 30*(4), 519–532. https://doi.org/10.1080/07294360.2010.512627

Mauroux, L., Dehler Zufferey, J., Rodondi, E., Cattaneo, A., Motta, E., & Gurtner, J. (2016). Writing reflective learning journals: Promoting the use of learning strategies and supporting the development of professional skills. *Writing for Professional Development.* https://doi.org/10.1163/9789004264830_007

2 Plumer, B., & Popovich, N. (2018). Here are the places that struggle to meet the rules on safe drinking water. *The New York Times.* https://www.nytimes.com/2018/02/12/climate/drinking-water-safety.html

Langin, K. (2018). Millions of Americans drink potentially unsafe tap water. How does your county stack up? Rural, low-income Americans are most at risk of consuming contaminants. *Science.* https://www.sciencemag.org/news/2018/02/millions-americans-drink-potentially-unsafe-tap-water-how-does-your-county-stack

3 Mische, Patricia M. (1991). Earth as peace teacher. In E. Boulding, C. Brigagao, & K. Clements (Eds.), *Peace, Culture and Society.* Boulder, CO: Westview Press. https://doi.org/10.4324/9780429301230

Scene 1

1 United Nations. (2019). Only 11 years left to prevent irreversible damage from climate change, speakers warn during general assembly high-level meeting: Ambition, urgency needed to address global emergency, Secretary General says. *United Nations General Assembly: Meetings Coverage.* https://www.un.org/press/en/2019/ga12131.doc.htm

Bearer, C. F., Molloy, E. J., Tessema, M. T. et al. (2022). Global climate change: The defining issue of our time for our children's health. *Pediatric Research.* https://doi.org/10.1038/s41390-022-02290-7

2 TED Radio Hour. (2020, August 21). *Lessons from the Summer.* [Interview with Tom Rivett-Carnac.]

3 Pearce, F. (2019). As climate change worsens, a cascade of tipping points looms. *Yale Environment 360.* https://e360.yale.edu/features/as-climate-changes-worsens-a-cascade-of-tipping-points-looms

4　World Health Organization. (2021). Climate change and health: Key facts. *World Health Organization.* https://www.who.int/news-room/fact-sheets/detail/climate-change-and-health

5　Carrington, D. (2022). "Monster monsoon": Why the floods in Pakistan are so devastating. *The Guardian.* https://www.theguardian.com/environment/2022/aug/29/monster-monsoon-why-the-floods-in-pakistan-are-so-devastating

6　Fraser, S. (2022). Pakistan floods are "a monsoon on steroids", warns UN chief. *BBC.* https://www.bbc.com/news/world-asia-62722117

7　Union of Concerned Scientists. (2023). Climate impacts: The consequences of climate change are already here. *Union of Concerned Scientists.* https://www.ucsusa.org/climate/impacts

8　CRED. (2023). EM-DAT: the international disaster database: Centre for research on the epidemiology of disasters. *Center for Research on the Epidemiology of Disasters: CRED.* Retrieved January 2023 from www.emdat.be

9　Klein, N. (2014). *This changes everything: Capitalism vs. the climate.* Penguin Random House.

10　Reuters. (2022). Key takeaways from the COP27 climate summit in Egypt. *Reuters.* https://www.reuters.com/business/cop/key-takeaways-cop27-climate-summit-egypt-2022-11-20/

11　European Environment Agency. (2022). Is Europe reducing its greenhouse gas emissions? *European Environment Agency.* Retrieved November 2022 from https://www.eea.europa.eu/themes/climate/eu-greenhouse-gas-inventory#:~:text=The%20EU%20has%20a%20set,were%2034%20%25%20below%201990%20levels.&text=Emissions%20have%20decreased%20in%20almost,industry%20and%20the%20residential%20sector

12　Weyler, R. (2022, June 1). The great carbon capture scam. *Greenpeace: Stories, Energy.* https://www.greenpeace.org/international/story/54079/great-carbon-capture-scam/

13　Abdulla, A., Hanna, R., Schell, K. R., Babacan, O., & Victor, D. G. (2021). Explaining successful and failed investments in US carbon capture and storage using empirical and expert assessments. *Environmental Research Letter, 16*(1), 014036. https://doi.org/10.1088/1748-9326/abd19e

14　Democracy Now. (2019). Why are some of Spain's biggest polluters sponsoring the U.N. climate summit? *Democracy Now.* https://www.democracynow.org/2019/12/6/big_polluters_sponsoring_cop25_climate_summit
Bousso, R. (2019). Big oil undermines U.N. climate goals with $50 billion of new projects: report. *Reuters.* https://www.reuters.com/article/us-climate-change-oil/big-oil-undermines-un-climate-goals-with-50-billion-of-new-projects-report-idUSKCN1VQ2WC

15　Smith, A. & Cannan, E. (1998). An inquiry into the nature and causes of the wealth of nations (E. Cannan, Ed.). *Electric Book Classics.* (Original work published 1776.)

16　Jackson, T. (2009). Prosperity without growth: Economics for a finite planet (1st ed.). *Routledge.* https://doi.org/10.4324/9781849774338

17 Taaliu, S. T. (2011). Indigenous knowledge, environment, and education in Africa. In J. Lin & R. Oxford (Eds.), *Transformative eco-education for human and planetary survival* (pp. 269–288). Information Age Publishing.

18 While there is a deep and long tradition of indigenous knowledge, wisdom, and community-building from around the world that could be covered in this section, such a review is beyond the scope of this book. The story we tell here about African Indigenous Knowledge was chosen due to our (Amanda and Jing's) personal access to information alone and is in no way an indication that we believe other traditions to be less interesting or applicable. We honor all traditions and believe that in them there are many answers.

19 McMichael, P. (1996). *Development and social change: A global perspective* (2nd ed.). Pine Forge Press.

20 UNCTAD. (2019). Economic development in Africa report 2019. *United Nations Conference on Trade and Development.* https://unctad.org/system/files/official-document/aldcafrica2019_en.pdf

21 Royte, E. (2006, August). Corn plastic to the rescue. *The Smithsonian.* https://www.smithsonianmag.com/science-nature/corn-plastic-to-the-rescue-126404720/

22 Lerner, S. (2019, July 20). Waste only: How the plastics industry is fighting to keep polluting the world. *The Intercept.* https://theintercept.com/2019/07/20/plastics-industry-plastic-recycling/

23 Plumber, B. (2006, May 22). *The origins of anti-litter campaigns.* Mother Jones. https://www.motherjones.com/politics/2006/05/origins-anti-litter-campaigns/
Dunaway, F. (2017, November 21). *The crying Indian ad that fooled the environment.* Chicago Tribune. https://www.chicagotribune.com/opinion/commentary/ct-perspec-indian-crying-environment-ads-pollution-1123-20171113-story.html

24 Hall, S. (2015). Exxon knew about climate change almost forty years ago: A new investigation shows the oil company understood the science before it became a public issue and spent millions to promote misinformation. *Scientific American.* scientificamerican.com/article/exxon-knew-about-climate-change-almost-40-years-ago/

25 Hotten, R. (2015, December 10). Volkswagen: The scandal explained. *BBC News.* https://www.bbc.com/news/business-34324772

26 Husock, H. (2020). The declining case of municipal recycling. *Manhattan Institute.* https://www.manhattan-institute.org/recycling-cost-benefit-analysis

27 American Recyclable Plastic Bag Alliance. (2022). https://bagalliance.org/

28 Klein, Naomi. (2014). *This changes everything: Capitalism vs. the climate.* Penguin Random House.

29 Rosemont, R. Jr. (2016, October 18). Capitalist ideology and the myth of the individual self, Part 1: Competing autonomous individual agents. *Huffington Post.* Retrieved November 2022 from https://www.huffpost.com/entry/capitalist-ideology-and-the-myth-of-the-individual-self-part-1_b_58065ff4e4b0dd54ce358acf

Rosemont, R. Jr. (2016, October 21). Capitalist ideology and the myth of the individual self, Part 2: Cooperating interrelated role-bearing persons. *Huffington Post*. https://www.huffpost.com/entry/capitalist-ideology-and-the-myth-of-the-individual-self-part-2_b_580a367be4b0cdea3d870608

30 Rosemont, R. Jr. (2016, October 21). Capitalist ideology and the myth of the individual self, Part 2: Cooperating interrelated role-bearing persons. *Huffington Post*. https://www.huffpost.com/entry/capitalist-ideology-and-the-myth-of-the-individual-self-part-2_b_580a367be4b0cdea3d870608

31 NPR. (2013, July 5). What is farm runoff doing to the water? Scientists wade in. *National Public Radio*. https://www.npr.org/sections/thesalt/2013/07/09/199095108/Whats-In-The-Water-Searching-Midwest-Streams-For-Crop-Runoff

32 UNEP. (2020, July 20). *10 Things You Should Know About Industrial Farming*. United Nations Environment Programme. Retrieved October 2022 from https://www.unep.org/news-and-stories/story/10-things-you-should-know-about-industrial-farming#:~:text=According%20to%20some%20estimates%2C%20industrialized,US%243%20trillion%20every%20year

33 Rockefeller Foundation. (2021, July). True cost of food: Measuring what matters to transform the U.S. food system (Executive Summary). *The Rockefeller Foundation*. Retrieved October 2022 from https://www.rockefellerfoundation.org/wp-content/uploads/2021/07/True-Cost-of-Food-Report-Executive-Summary-Final.pdf

34 U.S. Department of Agriculture. (2023). *Climate Change*. Economic Research Service: U.S. Department of Agriculture. Retrieved January 2023 from https://www.ers.usda.gov/topics/natural-resources-environment/climate-change/

35 Oxford, R. L. (2012). Eco-fashion. In J. Lin & R. Oxford (Eds.), *Transformative Eco-Education for Human and Planetary Survival* (pp. 269–288). Information Age Publishing.

36 Butler, S. (2018, December 19). Is fast-fashion giving way to the sustainable wardrobe? *The Guardian*. https://www.theguardian.com/business/2018/dec/29/fast-fashion-giving-way-sustainable-wardrobe

Scene 2

1 World Health Organization. (2021). *Air Pollution*. Retrieved February 14, 2023, from https://www.who.int/health-topics/air-pollution#tab=tab_1

2 Jacobo, J. (2019, February 2). Prison animal programs are benefitting both inmates and hard-to-adopt dogs in Florida, experts say: The TAILS program has saved more than 500 at-risk dogs. *ABC News*. https://abcnews.go.com/US/prison-animal-programs-benefitting-inmates-hard-adopt-dogs/story?id=60600864

3 Deziel, C. (2018, July 20). Animals that share human DNA sequences. *Sciencing*. https://sciencing.com/animals-share-human-dna-sequences-8628167.html

4 Quammen, D. (2020). I am scared all the time: Chimps and people are clashing in rural Uganda. *National Geographic*. Retrieved September 16, 2023, from https://www.nationalgeographic.co.uk/animals/2019/11/i-am -scared-all-time-chimps-and-people-are-clashing-rural-uganda

Scene 3

1 Mignolo, W. (2003). Globalization and the geopolitics of knowledge: The role of the humanities in the corporate university. *Views from the South*, *4*(1), 97–119.
   Alatas, S. F. (2003). Academic dependency and the global division of labour in the social sciences. *Current Sociology*, *51*(6), 599–613.

2 Henderson, D. (2021). American wilderness philosophy. *Internet Encyclopedia of Philosophy*. Retrieved July 2021 from https://iep.utm.edu/am-wild/#H1

3 Deloria, V. (2001). American Indians and the wilderness. In R. Bohannon (Ed.), *Religions and the environment: A reader in religion, nature and ecology* (pp. 85–92). Bloomsbury Academic.

4 Bai, H. (2009). Re-animating the universe: Environmental education and philosophical animism. In M. McKenzie, H. Bai, P. Hart, & B. Jickling (Eds.), *Fields of green: Restorying culture, environment, education* (pp. 135–151). Hampton Press.

5 Cornford, Francis MacDonald (Trans.). (1970). *The republic of Plato*. Oxford University Press.

6 Korten, D. C. (2015). *Change the story, change the future: A living economy for a living earth*. Berrett-Keohler Publishers Inc.

7 Lin, J. (2018). From self-cultivation to social transformation: The Confucian embodied pathways and educational implications. In Y. Liu & W. Ma (Eds.), *Confucianism and education* (pp. 169–182). State University of New York Press.

8 Lin, J. (2019). Enlightenment from body-spirit integration: Dunhuang's Buddhist cultivation pathways and educational implications. In D. Xu (Ed.), *The Dunhuang Grottos and global education: Philosophical, spiritual, scientific, and aesthetic insights* (pp. 113–132). Palgrave Macmillan.

9 Culham, T., & Lin, J. (2020). *Daoist cultivation of Qi and virtue for life, wisdom, and learning*. Palgrave Macmillan, Springer.

Scene 4

1 Mische, P. M. (1991). Earth as peace teacher. In E. Boulding, C. Brigagao, & K. Clements (Eds.), *Peace, culture and society*. Westview Press. https://doi.org/10.4324/9780429301230

2 Messenger, S. (2012). *Keeper of the lost cities: Book 1* (p. 98). Aladdin.

3 Lao Tzu. (400 BC/2019). Tao te ching – Lao Tzu – chapter 80. In Weed's (Ed.), *Tao Te Ching – Lao Tzu – a comparative study*. https://www.wussu.com/laotzu/laotzu80.html

4 Eisen, M. B. & Brown, P. O. (2022). Rapid global phaseout of animal agriculture has the potential to stabilize greenhouse gas levels for 30 years and offset 68 percent of CO2 emission this century. *PLOS Climate*. https://doi.org/10.1371/journal.pclm.0000010

   Than, K. (2022, February 1). Replacing animal agriculture and shifting to a plant-based diet could drastically curb greenhouse gas emissions, according to a new model. *Stanford News*. https://news.stanford.edu/2022/02/01/new-model-explores-link-animal-agriculture-climate-change/

5 Good Food Institute. (2021). https://gfi.org
   Impossible Foods. (2022). https://impossiblefoods.com

6 Stephens, N. & Ellis, M. (2020). Cellular agriculture in the UK: A review. *Wellcome Open Research*, *5*(12). https://doi.org/10.12688/wellcomeopenres.15685.2. PMID: 32090174; PMCID: PMC7014924.

7 New Harvest. (2023). What is cell ag: Cellular agriculture is the production of animal-sourced foods from cell culture. *New Harvest*. Retrieved February 15, 2023 from https://new-harvest.org/what-is-cellular-agriculture/

8 Byrne, B. & Murray, S. (2021). 2020 state of the industry report: Cultivated meat. *The Good Food Institute*. https://gfi.org/wp-content/uploads/2021/04/COR-SOTIR-Cultivated-Meat-2021-0429.pdf

9 Lankford, E. L. (1997). Ecological stewardship in art education. *Art Education*, *50*(6), pp. 47–53. Stable URL: http://links.jstor.org/sici?sici=0004-3125%28199711%2950%3A6%3C47%3AESIAE%3E2.0.CO%3B2-6

10 Thoreau, H. (2014). Walking. In R. Bohannon (Ed.), *Religions and environments* (pp. 19–30). Bloomsbury Publishing.

11 Emerson, R. W. (1844). *Nature*. American Transcendentalism Web. Retrieved November 2022 from https://www.vcu.edu/engweb/transcendentalism/authors/emerson/essays/nature1844.html

Scene 5

1 Forbes, J. D. (2001). Indigenous Americans: Spirituality and ecos. *Daedalus, Fall 2001*. https://www.amacad.org/publication/indigenous-americans-spirituality-and-ecos

2 The Parable of the Raft tells the story of a traveler who builds a raft to help him cross a river, then tries to carry it with him into the forest on the other side because it has been so useful. As he begins to toil with the heavy raft through the forest, the Buddha asks him if carrying the raft is a good idea. The parable is understood as articulating the Buddhist idea of "non-attachment": use the teachings to help you reach enlightenment, but do not cling to the teachings, lest they become a burden that only weighs you down.

3 Lin, J. (2019). Enlightenment from body-spirit integration: Dunhuang's Buddhist cultivation pathways and educational implications. In Di Xu (Ed.), *The Dunhuang Grottos and global education: Philosophical, spiritual, scientific, and aesthetic insights* (pp. 113–132). Palgrave-MacMillon (imprint), Springer Nature (publishing co).

4 Morgan, B. (2006). *Vision walk*. St. Lynn's Press.

5 Britannica, T. Editors of Encyclopedia. (2023, January 1). *Li Shizhen. Encyclopedia britannica*. https://www.britannica.com/biography/Li-Shizhen
     Nappi, C. (2010, January–February). Li Shizhen: Brief life of a pioneering naturalist: 1518–1593. *Harvard Magazine*. https://www.harvardmagazine.com/2010/01/pharmacologist-li-shizhen-biography

6 Warren, K. (1993). Introduction to ecofeminism. In M. E. Zimmerman, J. B. Callicott, G. Sessions, K. J. Warren, & J. Clark (Eds.), *Environmental philosophy: From animal rights to radical ecology* (pp. 253–267). Englewood Cliffs.

7 Lin, J. (2006). *Love, peace and wisdom in education*. Rowman & Littlefield.

8 Capra, F. (1999). *The tao of physics*. Boston: Shambhala.

9 Hahn, T. N. (1988/2009). *The heart of understanding: Commentaries on the Prajnaparamita Heart Sutra*. Parallox Press.

Interlude

1 Concomitantly, it bears mentioning that both colonialism and globalization have played significant roles in the creation of pockets of human deprivation around the world, like the one detailed here. Examining the enduring legacy of colonialism and the way globalized markets have thrust some countries into dire economic and social positions is beyond the scope of this book; nonetheless, it is a conversation hovering at the edges, which we want to acknowledge.

2 Lin, J. (2006). *Love, peace and wisdom in education: Vision for education in the 21st century*. Rowman & Littlefield Education.

Scene 6

1 Jankie300. (2014, March 13). *Urie Bronfenbrenner ecological theory* [video]. https://youtu.be/5htRhvm4iyI

2 Bettie, M. (2020). Exchange diplomacy: Theory, policy and practice in the Fulbright program. *Place Branding and Public Diplomacy, 16*(3), 212–223.
     Eller, A., Abrams, D., & Zimmermann, A. (2011). Two degrees of separation: A longitudinal study of actual and perceived extended international contact. *Group Processes & Intergroup Relations, 14*(2), 175–191. https://doi.org/10.1177/1368430210391120

Liu, E. & Hutt, E. (2021). The use of educational exchange and international education to improve US-sino relationship. *Journal of Student Research: High School Edition, 10*(2), 1–7. ISSN: 2167-1907.

3 Mills, C. W. (2007). White ignorance. In S. Sullivan & N. Tuana (Eds.), *Race and epistemologies of ignorance* (pp. 13–38). Suny Press.

4 Pesaresi, M., Melchiorri, M., Siragusa, A., & Kemper, T. (2016). Atlas of the human planet 2016: Mapping human presence on earth with the global human settlement layer. *European Commission: JRC Science for Policy Report.* https://doi.org/10.2788/582834. https://ghsl.jrc.ec.europa.eu/documents/Atlas_2016.pdf?t=1533911627

5 Monbiot, G. (2012, November 19). If children lose contact with nature they won't fight for it. *The Guardian.* http://www.theguardian.com/commentisfree/2012/nov/19/children-lose-contact-with-nature

6 Ritchie, H. & Roser, M.. (2018). Urbanization. *Our World in Data.* Retrieved July 28, 2020, from https://ourworldindata.org/urbanization#:~:text=Using%20these%20definitions%2C%20it%20reports,more%20than%206.1%20billion%20people).

7 Louv, R. (2006). *Last child in the woods: Saving our children from nature deficit disorder* (pp. 54–111). Algonquin Books of Chapel Hill.

8 The Guardian. (2016, July 27). Children spend only half as much time outside as their parents did. *The Guardian: Environment.* https://www.theguardian.com/environment/2016/jul/27/children-spend-only-half-the-time-playing-outside-as-their-parents-did

9 AACAP. (2020). Screen time and children. *American Academy of Child and Childhood Psychiatry.* aacap.org/AACAP/Families_and_Youth/Facts_for_Families/FFF-Guide/Children-And-Watching-TV-054.aspx

Scene 7

1 Feinberg, W. & Soltis, J. F. (2009). *School and society.* Teachers College Press.

2 LeFray, R. (2006). An ecological critique of education. *International Journal of Children's Spirituality, 11*(1), 35–45.

3 Xiaoyan, S. & Lin, J. (2012). Daoism and Chinese landscape painting. In J. Lin & R. Oxford (Eds.), *Transformative eco-education for human and planetary survival* (pp. 335–348). Information Age Publishing.

4 Chengqiang, Q., Ying, X., Yan, F., & Tian, L. (2018). Environmental education in China: A case study of four elementary and secondary schools. In G. Reis & J. Scott (Eds.), *International perspectives on the theory and practice of environmental education: A reader. Environmental discourses in science education* (Vol. 3). Springer. https://doi.org/10.1007/978-3-319-67732-3_13

Scene 8

1 Sun, X. & Lin, J. (2012). Daoism and Chinese landscape painting: Implication for environmental education. In J. Lin & R. Oxford (Eds.), *Transformative eco-education for human and planetary survival* (pp. 335–348). Information Age Publishing.

2 Zajonc, A. (2009). *Meditation as contemplative inquiry: When knowing becomes love.* Lindisfarne Books.

3 Barbezat, D. & Bush, M. (2014). *Contemplative practices in higher education: Powerful methods to transform teaching and learning.* Jossey-Bass. ISBN: 978-118-43527-4.

   Bai, H., et al. (2009). Contemplative pedagogy and revitalization of teacher education. *Alberta Journal of Educational Research, 55*(3), 319–334.

   Lin, J., Oxford, R., & Brantmeier, E. (2013). *Embodied pathways to wisdom and social transformation.* Information Age Publishing.

   Lin, J., Culham, T., & Edwards, S. (2018). *Contemplative pedagogies for transforming teaching, learning, and being.* Information Age Publishing.

   Keiser, D. L. (2013). Killing mosquitoes and keeping practice: teacher education as sustaining paradox. *Frontiers of Education in China, 8*(1), 28940. Print.

   Miller, J. P. (2013). *The contemplative practitioner: Meditation in education and the workplace* (2nd ed.). University of Toronto Press.

   Roth, H. (2006). Contemplative studies: Prospect for a new field. *Teachers College Record, 108*(9), 1787–1815.

4 Edwards, S. (2013). Using Hula to teach personal, interpersonal and environmental peace. In J. Lin, R. Oxford, & E. Brantmeier (Eds.), *Embodied pathways to wisdom and social transformation* (pp. 23–32). Information Age Publishing.

   Lin, J. (2006). *Development of integrated intelligence.* In *love, peace, and wisdom in education.* Rowman and Littlefield Education.

   Lin, J. (2013). Education for transformation and an expanded self: Paradigm shift for wisdom education. In J. Lin, R. L. Oxford, & E. J. Brantmeier (Eds.), *Re-Envisioning higher education: Embodied pathways to wisdom and social transformation* (pp. 23–32). Information Age Publishing.

5 Bai, H., Scott, C., & Donald, B. (2009). Contemplative pedagogy and revitalization of teacher education. *Alberta Journal of Educational Research, 55*(3), 319–334.

6 Zajonc, A. (2009). *Meditation as contemplative inquiry: When knowing becomes love.* Lindisfarne Books.

7 Miller, J. (2013). *The contemplative practitioner: Meditation in education and the workplace* (2nd ed.). University of Toronto Press. Print.

8 Lin, J., Culham, T., & Oxford, R. (2016). Developing a spiritual research paradigm: A Confucian perspective. In J. Lin, R. Oxford, & T. Culham (Eds.), *Toward a spiritual research paradigm: Exploring new ways of*

knowing, researching and being (pp. 141–169). Charlotte, NC: Information Age Publishing.

9 Fiore, A. (2018). The classroom as interconnected, living space: Integrating reflective, contemplative practice into general education. In J. Lin, T. Culham, & S. Edwards (Eds.), *Contemplative pedagogies for transforming teaching, learning, and being* (pp. 315–328). Information Age Publishing.

10 Komjathy, L. (2011). Field notes from a daoist professor. In J. Simmer-Brown & F. Grace (Eds.), *Meditation and the classroom: Contemplative pedagogy for religious studies* (pp. 95–103). State University of New York Press.

11 Xiaoyan, S. & Lin, J. (2012). Daoism and Chinese landscape painting. In J. Lin & R. Oxford (Eds.), *Transformative eco-education for human and planetary survival* (pp. 335–348). Information Age. Publishing.

12 Gray, P. (2017). Self-directed education—unschooling and democratic schooling. In *Oxford research encyclopedia of education*. Oxford University Press. https://doi.org/10.1093/acrefore/9780190264093.013.80

13 LeFray, R. (2006). An ecological critique of education. *International Journal of Children's Spirituality, 11*(1), 35–45.

14 Lin, J. (2006). *Love, peace and wisdom in education*. Rowman & Littlefield.

15 Rau, T. (2023, January 23). Sociocracy—basic concepts and principles. *Sociocracy For All*. https://www.sociocracyforall.org/sociocracy/

16 Louv, R. (2006). *Last child in the woods: Saving our children from nature-deficit disorder*. Algonquin Books of Chapel Hill.

17 Putney, D., Morris, R. C., & Sargent, P. R. (2015). Toward a green curriculum: Transforming the school house and classroom. In T. C. Chan, et al. (Eds.), *Marketing the green school: Form, function, and the future* (pp. 194–210). IGI Global.

18 Arao, B. & Clemens, K. (2013). From safe spaces to brave spaces: A new way to frame dialogue around diversity and social justice. In L. M. Landreman (Ed.), *The art of effective facilitation* (pp. 135–150). Stylus Publishing.

    Cabrera, N. L., Watson, J. S., & Franklin, J. D. (2016). Racial arrested development: A critical whiteness analysis of the campus ecology. *Journal of College Student Development 57*(2), 119–134.

    Kelly, B. T. & Gayles, J. G. (2015). Confronting systems of privilege and power in the classroom. In S. Watt (Ed.), *Designing transformative multicultural initiatives: Theoretical foundations, practical applications, and facilitator considerations* (pp. 164–179). Stylus Publishing.

    Watt, S. K. (2007). Difficult dialogues, privilege and social justice: Uses of the privileged identity exploration (pie) model in student affairs practice. *The College Student Affairs Journal, 26*(2), 114–126.

19 National Center for Education Statistics. (2021). Fast facts: Immediate transition to college. *National Center for Education Statistics*. Retrieved February 16, 2023, from https://nces.ed.gov/fastfacts/display.asp?id=51

20 The World Bank. (2022). School enrollment tertiary (% gross). *The World Bank*. Retrieved February 16, 2023, from https://data.worldbank.org/indicator/SE.TER.ENRR

21 Stewart, Mark. (2011). Greening the campus, culture, and curriculum. In J. Lin & R. Oxford (Eds.), *Transformative eco-education for human and planetary survival* (pp. 171–184). Information Age Publishing.

22 Second Nature. (2020). Mission. *Second Nature Climate Leadership Network*. https://secondnature.org/mission/

23 Second Nature. (n.d.). The presidents' climate leadership commitments: Climate leadership statement. *Second Nature Climate Leadership Network*. Retrieved February 16, 2023, from https://secondnature.org/signatory-handbook/the-commitments/

24 Sustainable UMD. (2023). Progress report. *The University of Maryland*. Retrieved February 16, 2023, from https://sustainability.umd.edu/progress/progress-report

25 UMD. (2018, November 29). UMD sustainability report marks significant climate action progress. *UMD Right Now*. Retrieved February 16, 2023, from https://umdrightnow.umd.edu/umd-sustainability-report-marks-significant-climate-action-progress

26 Earth Island Staff. Greening the ivory tower: Campuses Make sustainability a core curriculum. *Earth Island Journal,* 34–38. Retrieved February 16, 2023, from http://www.earthisland.org/journal/index.php/eij/article/greening_the_ivory_tower/

27 Cal State LA. (2020). Cal State LA hydrogen research and fueling facility (H2 Station). *California State University of LA*. Retrieved August 6, 2020, from www.https://Calstatela.edu/ecst/h2station

28 Tulane University. (2020). Nitrogen reduction challenge. *Tulane University*. Retrieved August 6, 2020, from www.https://taylor.tulane.edu/nitrogren-reduction-challenge/

29 Allen, E. & Patterson, B. (2019). Study finds West Virginia countries among "Worst in Nation" for drinking water violation. *West Virginia Public Broadcasting*. Retrieved August 6, 2020, from https://www.wvpublic.org/post/study-finds-west-virginia-counties-among-worst-nation-drinking-water-violations

Scene 9

1 Because I (Amanda) am a qualitative researcher whose work centers around the collecting, shaping, and telling of stories to create change, these pages draw primarily upon the work of psychologists and narrative researchers to understand and explain the power of story. However, it would be a disservice to those who came before not to stress that storytelling is, of course, as old as time. As such, there is a long, rich

history of scholarship that draws on both ancient and modern-day traditions, philosophies, and thought from the indigenous community, as well as from the work of racial justice scholars and activists. Much of their scholarship around the power of stories and storytelling echoes the main message of this book, yet is sadly beyond the scope of these pages (see endnote 3 for a brief reading list).

2 McAdams, D. P., Josselson, R., & Lieblich, A. (2011). *Identity and story: Creating self in narrative.* American Psychological Association.

3 Corntassel, J., Chaw-win-is, & Tlakwadzi (2009). Indigenous storytelling, truth-telling, and community approaches to reconciliation. *ESC: English Studies in Canada, 35*(1), 137–159. https://doi.org/10.1353/esc.0.0163

Fikile, N. (2015). Forest stories: Restorying encounters with the "natural" places in early childhood education. In V. Pacini-Ketchabaw & A. Taylor (Eds.), *Unsettling the colonial places and spaces of early childhood education* (1st ed.). Routledge. https://doi.org/10.4324/9781315771342

Tooth, R. & Renshaw, P. (2009). Reflections on pedagogy and place: A journey into learning for sustainability through environmental narrative and deep attentive reflection. *Australian Journal of Environmental Education, 25*, 95–104. https://doi.org/10.1017/S0814062600000434

Voyageur, C., Brearley, L., & Calliou, B. (2015). *Restorying indigenous leadership: Wise practices in community development.* Banff Centre Press.

4 Chase, S. (2018). Narrative Inquiry: Toward theoretical and methodological maturity. In N. K. Denzin & Y. S. Lincoln (Eds.), *The sage handbook of qualitative research* (5th ed., pp. 546–560). Sage Publications.

Clandinin, D. J. (2006). Narrative inquiry: A methodology for studying lived experience. *Research Studies in Music Education, 27*, 44–54.

Clandinin, D. J. (2013). *Engaging in narrative inquiry.* Routledge.

Josselson, R. (2011). Narrative research: Constructing, deconstructing, and reconstructing story. In F. J. Wertz, K. Charmaz, L. M. McMullen, R. Josselson, R. Anderson, & E. McSpadden (Eds.), *Five ways of doing qualitative analysis: Phenomenological psychology, grounded theory, discourse analysis, narrative research, and intuitive inquiry* (pp. 224–242). The Guilford Press.

Kirk, G. & Okazawa-Rey, M. (2018). Identities and social locations: Who am I? Who are my people? In M. Adams, W. J. Blumenfeld, D. C. J. Catalano, K. S. DeJong, H. W. Hackman, L.E. Hopkins, B.J. Love, M.L. Peters, D. Shalsko, & X. Zuniga (Eds.) *Readings of diversity and social justice* (4th ed.). Routledge.

Sparrow, L. M. (2000). Beyond multicultural man: Complexities of identity. *International Journal of Intercultural Relations, 24*(2), 173–201.

5 Wertz, F. J., Charmaz, K., McMullen, L. M., Josselson, R., Anderson, R., & McSpadden, E. (2011). *Five ways of doing qualitative analysis: Phenomenological psychology, grounded theory, discourse analysis, narrative research, and intuitive inquiry.* The Guilford Press.

6 McAdams, D. P., Josselson, R., & Lieblich, A. (2011). *Identity and story: Creating self in narrative.* American Psychological Association.

7 Chase, S. (2018). Narrative inquiry: Toward theoretical and methodological maturity. In N. K. Denzin & Y. S. Lincoln (Eds.), *The sage handbook of qualitative research* (5th ed., pp. 546–560). Sage Publications.
Clandinin, D. J. (2013). *Engaging in narrative inquiry.* Routledge.
Josselson, R. (2011). Narrative research: Constructing, deconstructing, and reconstructing story. In F. J. Wertz, K. Charmaz, L. M. McMullen, R. Josselson, R. Anderson, & E. McSpadden (Eds.), *Five ways of doing qualitative analysis: Phenomenological psychology, grounded theory, discourse analysis, narrative research, and intuitive inquiry* (pp. 224–242). The Guilford Press.

8 Tappan, M. B. (2006). Reframing internalized oppression and internalized domination: From the psychological to the sociocultural. *Teachers College, 10*(10), 2115–2144.

9 De St. Aubin, E., Wandrei, M., Skerven, K., & Coppolillo, C. M. (2006). A narrative exploration of personal ideology and identity. In D. P. McAdams, R. Josseslon, & A. Lieblich (Eds.), *Identity and story: Creating self in narrative* (pp. 223–248). American Pyschological Association.

10 Whittle, A., Mueller, F., & Mangan, A. (2009). Storytelling and "character": Victims, villains and heroes in the case of technological change. *Sagepub Journals, 16*(3), 425–442.
Bell, J. S. (2002) Narrative inquiry: More than just telling stories. *TESOL Quarterly, 36*(2), 207–213.

11 Josselson, R. (2011). Narrative research: Constructing, deconstructing, and reconstructing story. In F. J. Wertz, K. Charmaz, L. M. McMullen, R. Josselson, R. Anderson, & E. McSpadden (Eds.), *Five ways of doing qualitative analysis: Phenomenological psychology, grounded theory, discourse analysis, narrative research, and intuitive inquiry* (pp. 224–242). The Guilford Press.

12 Hinyard, L. J. & Krueter, M. W. (2007). Using narrative communication as a tool for health behavior change: A conceptual, theoretical, and empirical overview. *Health Education & Behavior, 34*(5), pp. 777–792. https://doi.org/10.1177/1090198106291963

13 Waters, S. (2015). Identity in the empathic community: Alcoholics anonymous as a model community for storytelling and change. *Pastoral Psychology, 64,* 769–782.

14 Angus, L. & Hardtke, K. (2007). Margaret's story: An intensive case analysis of insight and narrative process change in client-centered psychotherapy. *Insight in Psychotherapy* (1st ed., pp. 187–205).

INDEX

Page numbers followed with "n" refer to endnotes.